HIGH AND RISING

HIGH AND RISING

A BOOK ABOUT DE LA SOUL

MARCUS J. MOORE

DEYST.
An Imprint of William Morrow

DEYST.

HarperCollins books may be purchased for educational, business,
or sales promotional use. For information, please email the Special
Markets Department at SPsales@harpercollins.com.

FIRST EDITION

Designed by Alison Bloomer
Illustrations by Demont Pinder

Library of Congress Cataloging-in-Publication Data has been applied for.

ISBN 978-0-358-49488-1

24 25 26 27 28 LBC 5 4 3 2 1

TO MY MOTHER, DELORES, MY FIRST LOVE

C☮NTENTS

PROLOGUE

WEBSTER HALL WAS PACKED, SOME FANS YOUNGER, LESS JADED, others a little grayer with more dust on their birth certificates. It was the second of March, 2023. Dave had been gone for two weeks. The reality hadn't set in yet: the heartbeat of De La Soul, the big brother of alternative hip-hop, had died. Even now that's hard to fathom. I could tell it was tough for everyone else too. Certain people you just figure will be around for a long time.

It was the kind of party Dave would've liked: everyone was there to have fun, to celebrate him and the group and rap all the old songs without the weight of music industry bullshit dimming De La's light. Surely there was sadness, but not pity, like there had been in recent years. No more poor De La. After a long and arduous fight, the guys had reacquired the rights to their music, which meant new listeners would finally get to hear what we fell in love with in the 1980s, and older ones would get to hear it in a new context. It looked like Pos and Maseo were overwhelmed, like they wanted to cry but couldn't (or wouldn't) summon the tears publicly. But that's the thing about grief: it doesn't always arrive when you think it will, when others are grieving. Instead, there's this need to be strong, to make sure others are good. The grief lands privately when no one else is looking, when you hear their favorite songs or stumble across an old photo you didn't know existed. The grief can cripple and render you helpless. It can arise through the strum of a guitar, in the thud of a piano chord.

These things can trigger the past—the blessed visions and the dour ones—and the only thing you can do is lean into the emotion.

On the one hand, this was a celebration. When was the last time we'd seen Queen Latifah, Monie Love, Common, and Prince Paul together on the same stage? On the other, it was a memorial. And that was the toughest pill to swallow. Dave was supposed to be there, reciting his verses on "Stakes Is High" or "Plug Tunin'" with a baseball hat resting lazily atop his bushy black hair. We wanted to see him front and center, grinning through gapped teeth, appreciating the love billowing within the space. It would've been cool to see him rapping back and forth with Pos or with Queen and Monie. It would've been great to see him and his creative brothers count down to midnight together, to see the looks on their faces when the reality set in that their music was finally streaming and that they would finally profit (as much as one could profit from streaming in 2023) from all that hard work. It took too long to get the business straight, and Dave dying around that time felt incredibly unfair.

I still remember the Instagram Live chat announcing it in 2021. There was Dave in an orange Diadora brand T-shirt, staring into a screen, his face relieved and bewildered. His scraggly goatee pointed past the neck of his garment, and there were sprinkles of gray hair on his throat, on the top of his skull, and in his mustache. But it still looked like Dave, like Trugoy the Dove. He still had the same hairline, and his voice had the same lilt of years past when he chastised monetary excess and lackluster MCs. "I can't believe this," he said, shaking his head at no one in particular.

Seconds later, a new screen popped up beneath his face: it was Pos, another member of De La, walking through what looked to be a backstage area. As always, his beard was manicured and his head clean shaven, the same look he's sported for the past twenty-five years after his Afro went south. Unlike Dave, whose demeanor felt more relaxed, Pos was stone-faced, serious but not menacing.

He laughed and smiled, seemingly at Dave, who didn't have social media and looked uncomfortable running De La's official account. "The cat's out the bag, everybody's been talking about it for the last couple of days," Dave continued. "We have finally come down to a deal between ourselves and Reservoir Media to release our music in 2021. We're trying to work hard and diligently, along with the good folks at Reservoir, to get this done."

Over the previous two decades, De La's music had been trapped in digital purgatory, unavailable on streaming services due to sample clearance issues and an outdated contract with their former label, Tommy Boy Records. There had been false hope in recent years, first in 2018 when the label released vinyl of the group's third album, *Buhloone Mindstate*, and a year later when Tommy Boy executives vowed to do right by the group, only to propose a deal that wasn't in De La's best interest. But on this call, none of that mattered; it was finally time to breathe. There had been an entire generation of listeners who didn't know what classic De La sounded like. They could hear the band's later albums—2004's *The Grind Date* and 2016's *and the Anonymous Nobody . . .*—but much of their catalog, namely the definitive albums from '89 to '96, hadn't been heard beyond bootlegs, expensive vinyl, and YouTube rips. While this lent a "You had to be there" essence to De La's music, the band missed out on thousands, if not millions, of dollars in potential earnings.

The group wasn't on Instagram to wallow in the past; that had been well documented through articles, blog posts, and hearsay. Rather, the news being shared represented a way forward. The band had endured three decades of hardships in the music business. De La built up years of goodwill by putting out groundbreaking music that stayed true to their intuition. No matter the trend, and despite the pressure to create commercially viable art, they always went against the grain, building a sizable cult following in the process.

The IG Live was messy at first, but Dave and Pos were clear-eyed and eloquent when speaking on the group's dealings. Their laid-back easiness made it feel like you were FaceTiming with your uncles. Nearly halfway into the chat, the third and most spirited member of De La Soul arrived—Maseo, a DJ and producer whose big laugh and sometimes gruff demeanor made him the band's lovable mascot. He came into the talk as only he could: jovial, wearing big blue sunglasses and a sandy brown beard with pointed strands that looked like they'd been struck by lightning. "The record business is not really into giving artists back their catalog," he declared. "This just happened to be one of those unique situations based on what we've gone through." He then proceeded to give a brief history lesson on the music industry, before Dave cut through the chatter: "I'm looking forward to this relationship with you," he said to his bandmates. "We got twenty more years."

The height of De La's popularity came in 1989, when, following the release of their highly anticipated debut album, *3 Feet High and Rising*, they performed the recording's meteoric fifth single "Me Myself and I" on *The Arsenio Hall Show*. The pinnacle of Black achievement was appearing on the popular late-night TV program, whose guest list included a who's who of music and Hollywood: Whoopi Goldberg, Eddie Murphy, and Quincy Jones, to name a few. So for De La Soul, an upstart rap trio from the New York City suburbs, to make it there, they had to have something special. And they did. The group had just released *3 Feet High* to decent sales and widespread critical acclaim, and that was a chance to bring their intricate blend of rap to a national television audience.

But if they thought they'd have an ally in Arsenio, they quickly learned otherwise. Standing among the audience in a sleek gray suit, holding the *3 Feet High* album cover in his left hand, Arsenio dissed De La—albeit not on purpose. "I like to call 'em the hippies of hip-hop," he said with a big oblivious smile. This wasn't the first time this term was applied to the group. They even rejected it in the song they performed on *Arsenio*. By then, journalists had already rendered a judgment based on the bright colors and daisies with which they were often associated. Yet the term "hippy" relegated them to second-class stature; no matter how popular they were, it implied that they were a novelty, a joke, nothing more than a shiny new toy. Though they were pissed at Arsenio, the group didn't show it.

Arsenio conveyed what many people felt. No one expected De La Soul to be this successful—not the label they were signed to, not even the group members themselves. That's because they existed at a time when rappers had to exhibit conventional cool. They didn't portray themselves as gangsters like N.W.A or smooth-talking ladies' men like Big Daddy Kane or LL Cool J. Instead, De La appealed to the Black alternative, to those who liked rap but also liked jazz and punk and maybe owned a skateboard or played an instrument in the school band. They spoke to those who didn't conform to what Black was supposed to be. They made it cool for rappers to be nerdy and weird, to be seen as they are and not care about being judged. Because their music was equally positive and psychedelic and their album art and music videos were full of flowers and peace signs, the "hippy" title stuck. It also didn't help that the group had a song called "D.A.I.S.Y. Age" (short for "Da Inner Sound, Y'all"), which made listeners think about the late '60s, free love, and Woodstock. "I appreciate how and why it happened, but it wasn't the correct interpretation of our music's soul," Maseo once said. They wanted listeners to focus on the dexterity of their work, not the wild hairstyles and colorful clothes: "De La has always been about hip-hop. It's not about daisies or the hippy era. We were doing hip-hop our way."

DE LA SOUL WERE VICTIMS OF THEIR OWN SUCCESS. *3 FEET HIGH* WAS SUCH A smash hit that the following three albums couldn't measure up commercially or critically. Sure, the group had a dedicated fan base and the media still loved them, but the late-night appearances dwindled and the record sales trended downward. They wanted to be seen as serious musicians, but for certain listeners they'd always be the fun-loving guys who made palatable rap for maladjusted cul-de-sac kids. Despite the sonic complexity of their music, some simply couldn't move past the groundbreaking nature of "Plug Tunin'," "Potholes in My Lawn," and "Me Myself and I." Some fans wanted that again and again and wouldn't let De La move on. The group wanted to shed the labels given to them, to be somewhere in a studio listening to records, brainstorming the next creative wrinkle. But because they became so famous so quickly, there were greater demands on their time, and those moments of peace were fewer. Following the release of *3 Feet High*, the trio stayed on the road for the better part of a year, performing to packed arenas across the United States. The grind became a burden and created tension between the group and their label. The strain—exacerbated by mistrust regarding a sampling debacle on *3 Feet High*—lasted until 2021, when the two sides finally parted ways.

As they wrestled with prescribed imagery that didn't match their creative passion, they were soon besieged by bigger problems. In 1991, Howard Kaylan and Mark Volman—of the '60s rock band the Turtles—sued De La for $1.7 million, citing copyright infringement for using their song "You Showed Me" without permission. Sampling in rap music wasn't new then. In its infancy, DJs and beatmakers mined old soul and funk records for distinctive drum grooves to repurpose. Rap's most famous song, 1979's "Rapper's Delight" by the Sugarhill Gang, is little more than a loop of the hit song "Good Times" by the funk band Chic. Throughout the '80s, you couldn't go a few songs without hearing the recrafted drum breaks of James Brown collaborator Clyde Stubblefield, whose solo on Brown's 1970 track "Funky Drummer" is reportedly the most sampled break of all time. Rap music *was* sampling, and De La molded the technique into its own art form. *3 Feet High* combined more than sixty sampled vocal and audio clips from the likes of the Monkees, Michael Jackson, and Liberace, which gave the album a polychromatic sound with multiple entry points. When coupled with the group's comedic skits, inside jokes, and witty banter, it felt like we were eavesdropping on private chats between De La and their producer, Prince Paul. It was rap with a broad sonic palette, the likes of which hadn't been attempted before, setting the blueprint for like-minded artists to follow. Never before had we heard an album with such a vast array of genres represented within the context of hip-hop.

The lawsuit called the art of sampling into question. "Sampling is just a longer term for theft," Volman once said. "Anybody who can honestly say sampling is some sort of creativity has never done anything creative." His jab condemned rap music as a whole. In the genre's earliest days, when observers believed it was just a passing craze, established artists looked the other way as beatmakers manipulated their music for this new sound. But as rap grew in popularity and its songs rose up the Billboard charts, some older musicians sought financial compensation for their art being used in this way. With all the lawsuits being filed, many of which were settled out of court, some thought rap would be stamped out before it really got started.

While the De La case was the most egregious example of copyright infringement in rap, it wasn't the first. Four years prior, in 1987, the funk musician Jimmy Castor sued Beastie Boys for using the phrase "Yo, Leroy" from his song "The Return of Leroy (Part 1)" on their first album's lead single, "Hold It Now, Hit It." Stetsasonic, a Brooklyn-based rap group also produced by Prince Paul and signed to Tommy Boy, paid the jazz keyboardist Lonnie Liston Smith three thousand dollars to sample the bass line of "Expansions" for their song "Talkin' All That Jazz." Before the Turtles lawsuit, the label cut deals with other artists sampled on *3 Feet High*, most notably with Funkadelic founder and lead singer George Clinton for the use of his band's "(Not Just) Knee Deep" for De La's "Me Myself and I," supposedly paying one hundred thousand dollars for the sample. Reportedly, the Turtles were offered one thousand dollars after *3 Feet High*'s release. Tommy Boy claimed the sample for "You Showed Me" had been manipulated to the point where the new work—in the song "Transmitting Live from Mars"—sounded nothing like the original.

Behind the scenes, tensions started mounting between De La and Tommy Boy. Not only did the group disagree with the way they were marketed, but the Turtles debacle widened the gap between the two factions. The label founder, Tom Silverman, said the band didn't tell them about the sample. "We would've just left it off if we had known," he once said. "But we didn't even know that was on there and they figured no one would care." Maseo put the onus on Tommy Boy. "When we first released our debut, we followed all the requirements to hand in sample clearances and make sure things were dealt with," he once told Red Bull Music Academy. "All we had to do is fill out the forms and hand them in, but they were in control of the administration, so they felt like certain things like 'Transmitting Live from Mars' was insignificant to clear because it was just such a small skit. Who's going to really pay attention to something so silly as that?" The case was settled out of court for an undisclosed amount. A few years later, De La started jabbing Tommy Boy on their songs.

BY 1996, AS RAP MUSIC MOVED FROM STONEHEARTED STREET TALES TO MORE decadent fare, De La Soul's career teetered. The trio had spent the past few years debunking preconceived notions of who they were and how they were supposed to sound. Their sophomore album, 1991's *De La Soul Is Dead*, was a sardonic response to hippy culture, the Arsenio diss, record label nonsense, and rappers who thought De La were soft (and learned the hard way that they weren't). The sound was darker and the tone was cynical, as if De La had already grown tired of the industry rat race. By the time *Buhloone Mindstate* was released in 1993, personal turmoil between them and their collaborators began to surface. In turn, the music emitted a muted, jazz-inflected aura, and the lyrics were equally gloomy and combative. And where *De La Soul Is Dead* succeeded commercially, *Buhloone Mindstate* was lauded by music journalists but didn't sell well. They were still critical darlings, but there were new voices on the horizon and De La's didn't ring as loudly. Groups like Wu-Tang Clan and A Tribe Called Quest pulled bigger audiences and sold more records; on the West Coast, rappers Dr. Dre and Snoop Doggy Dogg perfected gangsta rap, a subgenre with raunchy lyrics and glossy, Funkadelic-sampling beats. Other acts like Nas and Mobb Deep were also on the come-up, their music just as sordid as Dre's or Wu-Tang's, although it eschewed the pitfalls of Compton and Staten Island for the drug trade in Queens.

De La's attitude didn't help their cause, though. They were beginning to vocalize how they felt about hip-hop's new wave—namely the "shiny-suit era," ushered in by the record mogul Sean "Puff Daddy" Combs—and they weren't shy about expressing how all the champagne popping, tailored clothing, and drug narratives were hurting the culture. "I'm sick of bitches shakin' asses," Dave declared on "Stakes Is High," the statement-setting lead single from their album of the same name. "I'm sick of talkin' about blunts, sick of Versace glasses . . . sick of half-ass awards shows, sick of name-brand clothes." He doubled down on "Itsoweezee (Hot)," a solo track from *Stakes Is High*: "See them Cubans don't care what y'all niggas do / Colombians ain't never ran with your crew." They weren't alone in their condemnation of this corner of the genre—plenty of other artists felt similarly—but De La sounded grumpy, like they were wagging fingers at the new school for not doing it like them. In years past, they would've injected humor into the dig, but after seven years in the business and all the battles they endured, De La was fed up. Hip-hop culture had strayed too far from the creative diversity of its origins; now, the sound was homogenized and too focused on opulence.

Their target moved from rappers to Tommy Boy. At first the quips were cheeky yet lighthearted, a subtle lyric here and there. But before long, De La and Tommy Boy would be locked in a bitter legal dispute over streaming rights, a decades-long battle that held their music captive. De La Soul—once considered one of the brightest acts in the business—had fallen into obscurity.

It's easy to look back and wonder how it came to this, but conversations with peers from that era suggest the relationship between De La and Tommy Boy was frayed from the start. Success covered the wounds initially, but as hip-hop changed and the group refused to conform, the gashes only deepened. In turn, De La's fall wasn't steep or sudden; it was a long, slow descent. That's not to negate the group's lasting impact. Even as their output slowed, and their later albums didn't have the same oomph, they were still just as beloved. There's no in-between with De La: if you know their music, you love it and them; they've always been the guys you wanted to see win.

IF YOU WANT TO KNOW HOW IMPORTANT DE LA SOUL IS TO HIP-HOP, CONSIDER the music that likely wouldn't exist without them. There's no Mos Def, Common, or the Roots. No Pharrell, Kanye West, or Kendrick Lamar. That's not to say these artists didn't find creative inspiration elsewhere, but at a time when rappers presented themselves as screw-faced thug dudes, De La dared to be different: their music prioritized fun and togetherness in an industry that didn't always lend itself to such excitement. Without their courage, a young Mos wouldn't have felt seen as a budding rapper and actor living in Bed-Stuy. The Roots would have thought their acoustic jazz-rap hybrid was too wonky to make noise. Perhaps Kanye would've thought twice about wearing a pink polo shirt on the South Side of Chicago. De La brought freedom to hip-hop, and some thirty years after their introduction, there's still so much to unravel about their artistic genius. Despite their financial missteps and their sometimes overly critical appraisal of the culture, De La Soul is a Mount Rushmore group that, regardless of burgeoning trends, prioritized purity and remained true to their art.

They also made me feel embraced as a young Black boy growing up in Landover, Maryland, a small suburban town alongside the northeastern border of Washington, DC. I was eight years old when I saw the grainy video for "Potholes in My Lawn." The song's dizziness caught me off guard. The beat didn't progress as much as it stumbled, the tempo pitched down and off-centered to emulate a drunken stupor. Then there were these guys with these weird hairstyles. They looked like my older cousins and spoke just like me. The rhymes weren't fast or technically precise; they felt conversational, like Pos and Dave were talking to me directly. It was all quite foreign, no hypermasculine rappers with gold chains and athletic jackets yelling for no reason. These cats seemed regular yet different, alien in the way they approached rhythm and style. There was yodeling on the song—*yodeling?!*—and the sense of community seemed palpable in the video. Right away, I wasn't so strange. I could listen to rap and R&B and not feel odd about watching Madonna and David Bowie videos on MTV. De La's music and stylistic choices proved they felt the same.

Within these pages, we will see them go from naive high school students who saw rap as a cool thing to try after class to legendary musicians with legions of admirers across the world. *High and Rising* doesn't just tell the story of De La Soul; it unpacks the birth of hip-hop and the evolution of alternative rap. It's also a memoir about my own travels through life and the environment, and how their music helped me grow as a person and creator in a landscape that doesn't always understand differing viewpoints of artistry. I wanted to write from a critical lens and a fan's perspective, to speak to people like me who have De La to thank for their own expression. *High and Rising* acknowledges the band's impact without ignoring the missteps. This is a conversation. De La isn't infallible; it was important to be honest about their errors, just like we'd do privately.

When discussing any artist, the human element is important. One must know the environment that birthed this creativity and the external circumstances that bolstered it. So for De La, that means examining the history of Amityville and the Black sections of Long Island as an artistic hub. While the suburb didn't have the same pop as neighboring New York City, some of rap's all-time greats are from there. Rakim, EPMD, and MF DOOM are all Long Island natives who helped shape the genre from the '80s to the present day. *High and Rising* is a cultural biography that not only contextualizes the rise, prominence, and legacy of De La Soul but assesses their impact through a first-person standpoint based on my own context and decades-long career covering music. The group didn't participate in this book, but through new interviews with other collaborators, research, and my own memory, we learn that the group's creative freedom was both off-putting and liberating. Former Tommy Boy employees discuss the seismic impact of De La's early years and the simmering beef between the group and the label. Mike G and Afrika Baby Bam of Jungle Brothers walk us through the creation of the heavily influential Native Tongues collective, which featured members of De La, A Tribe Called Quest, and the JBs and forged a path for similar collectives to follow decades later.

Far too often, Black artists like De La Soul go on not knowing the impression they've made. Hip-hop is thought to be a young person's culture; when our pioneers sprout a few grays or lose some hair, we look for the next thing that reminds us of them without acknowledging the source. Then something unfortunate happens and we lament their not getting the love they deserved. De La Soul are a celebrated crew that deserve widespread adoration right now and always. They are history—Black history, American history, world history, my history, and yours. They're a living, breathing organism and a sound. Men who made it cool to be fans, to feel, to chuckle, to give big hugs and tell other grown Black men you love them. That was revolution. *High and Rising* tells the whole story—the positive, the negative, the self-inflicted distress, and the eventual redemption of the band and myself. It meditates on death and subsequent grief, navigating the push and pull of bereavement as life moves forward. This isn't just a hip-hop tale, though of course that would be enough; it's a book about staying the course, and how holding true to your virtue can lead to dynamic results.

FROM STRONG ISLAND, WITH LOVE

OME FORTY MILES EAST FROM NEW YORK CITY ALONG I-495, PAST John F. Kennedy International Airport, Hempstead, and Massapequa, sits a suburban enclave known more for a grisly murder, and the horror movie franchise it spawned, than its hip-hop scene. When certain people hear the name Amityville, they think of the cozy Dutch colonial home at 112 Ocean Avenue where, on November 13, 1974, Ronald DeFeo Jr. killed his parents and four siblings as they slept in their beds. The incident led locals to believe the house was possessed; author Jay Anson published a novel about this in 1977 called *The Amityville Horror*. A litany of films followed. The town is also where one of hip-hop's most iconoclastic bands got its start, away from the glitz and bravado of the big city, the birthplace and epicenter of a culture that was still finding its way. In Amityville Memorial High School, a massive edifice along Merrick Road with a distinguished golden eagle statue guarding its entrance, students David Jolicoeur, Kelvin Mercer, and Vincent Mason Jr. were laying the foundation for a rap group that would surprise the world.

Their neighborhood didn't lend itself to the hardscrabble narrative attached to New York City rappers. Amityville was a quiet, middle-class area. In New York City, a sprawling concrete labyrinth known for its fast-paced hustle, you didn't live there—you endured it. That was especially true in the 1970s, as violent crime and economic hardship made the region dangerous to inhabit. In Amityville, though, you could buy or rent houses that had lawns and were in close proximity to Great South Bay. "There wasn't that clutter of everyone living on top of one another," Mercer once said. "You didn't have the mass of apartments and project buildings. Of course there were bad areas in Long Island. You get those everywhere. However, we were very different from the kids in, say, Brooklyn or the Bronx or Harlem. Naturally it influenced our music and our lyrics." In the mid-'80s, the crack cocaine epidemic hit Long Island just as hard as it hit cities like Chicago, Detroit, and Washington, DC. Crack dealers from New York City would travel over and converge at the intersection of Albany Avenue and Great Neck Road in North Amityville to sell drugs, making it a bastion of crime on Long Island.

Though rap was a developing genre, Long Island already had a history of producing great talent. Chuck D, the lead vocalist of the pro-Black rap outfit Public Enemy, grew up in Roosevelt and met his rapping partner William Drayton—aka Flavor Flav—at Adelphi University in Suffolk County. Rakim, an innovative rapper whose rhythmic flow emulated jazz scales and influenced generations of MCs after him, is from Wyandanch. Jolicoeur, Mercer, and Mason would be different. Though Public Enemy and Rakim were groundbreaking acts, they still fit the parameters of what constituted rap at the time. Where they had the steely resolve and wore fashionable clothes, Jolicoeur, Mercer, and Mason looked like bohemians who shopped at the thrift store. But to write them off simply because they didn't look like rappers would've been a misjudgment of character. They were raised on Long Island, but their roots were planted in the city.

Mercer's family moved to Massapequa from the South Bronx in 1979, just as hip-hop was beginning to take shape under dire circumstances there. Throughout the 1970s, with the city in economic peril, landlords paid arsonists to burn their own properties to collect insurance money. The practice hit the Bronx the hardest; by the time the Mercers moved out of their apartment on 169th Street, their building, a massive brown brick facade like other projects in New York, was the only one left standing on the block. "We had this crazy landlord and we were always having fires in our building," Mercer recalled. "And it came out later it was our landlord torching our building." The elder Mercers wanted a better life for their children, so they trekked to Harlem for a year as they prepared for long-term residence on Long Island. Kelvin, an introverted preteen, adjusted well to the new scenery. His parents used to send him and his brothers to Waynesboro, Georgia (his mother's hometown), in the summer months to get away from the tensions of city living. So life on Long Island, with its slower pace, offered the perfect backdrop for a naturally reserved kid to write short stories in his bedroom and absorb the music his father played on the hi-fi stereo.

Kelvin, a dark-skinned boy with big, piercing eyes, was introduced to music by his father, Garland, a North Carolina–born vocalist who used to sing around the house and in the church choir. He loved rock and roll, soul, and jazz, and in school he sang love songs in doo-wop groups. That infatuation with music followed him into fatherhood, where Kelvin stood beside him as a young boy and watched his dad spin Motown 45s. In turn, Kelvin grew fascinated with the sounds he heard, took up singing, and even spent time in the church choir himself. But Kelvin soon took an interest in rap, like a lot of young Black kids in the early '80s. No longer did he just want to hear what his father played; acts like the Sugarhill Gang and Grandmaster Flash and the Furious Five became his new obsession. "I would hear my brother talking about a cassette they had with someone rhyming on it. I didn't know at the time that it was Cold Crush Brothers or Fantastic Romantic 5," Mercer recalled. "That was my initial understanding of hip-hop. My older brothers would be talking to my cousin about it." He gave up singing for good and tried his hand at DJing and rapping.

In 1985, as a high school sophomore, he met Jolicoeur, a husky kid in the eleventh grade with caramel-colored skin and dreadlocks who had moved to Long Island from Brooklyn with his Haitian parents. They became fast friends through a shared love of hip-hop, and stood out because they were quirky and operated in their own universe. They had a palpable charm that others were drawn to, and they were brave enough to stick to their singularity, even when close friends took to popular trends. They shaved peace signs and lightning bolts into their hair and spoke in their own secret language. Even in an era where lots of people experimented with identity, Mercer and Jolicoeur were conspicuous; that way of being stayed with them through adulthood.

Back then, though, neither one of them rapped publicly. Shortly after they met, they joined the local rap group Easy Street, where Mercer DJed under the name DJ Soundsop and Jolicoeur beatboxed. But the other rappers weren't as serious about making it a career, so Mercer and Jolicoeur split from the crew and decided to keep working together, sustaining the creative synergy they had developed. They linked with a respected DJ in town named Charlie Rock, who worked all the top parties and knew everyone in the close-knit scene. Rock was from Jamaica, Queens, and moved to Long Island as a ninth grader, where he was in the marching band with Rakim at Wyandanch High School. Rock lived in North Amityville, just around the corner from Jolicoeur, and knew his older brother, Michael. "One day Mike goes, 'Hey, my brother can rap.' I was like, 'Your brother can't rap, man,'" Rock told me. "Dave said some rhymes and they were actually dope." He and Jolicoeur started working on music together, then Mercer came through at Jolicoeur's behest. The first iteration of De La Soul was born.

History has given all the credit to Jolicoeur, Mercer, Mason, and their producer "Prince Paul" Huston for conceptualizing the group's sound and artistic focus, yet Rock was there in the beginning—before Mercer, Mason, and Huston—brainstorming ideas and finding esoteric songs to sample. In Rock's house, they dug for unconventional sounds that didn't fit what was being repurposed in rap music at the time. Everything from alt-rock to folk was on the table. "The core of developing that shit was me and Dave," Rock told me of De La's earliest days. He even helped come up with what became the group's slogan: "the D.A.I.S.Y. Age," an acronym meaning "Da Inner Sound, Y'all," that was supposed to encapsulate the group's joyful aesthetic. Rock and Jolicoeur's version was R-rated and didn't align with the image laid out for the group later. "People would be like, 'the D.A.I.S.Y. Age,'" he continued, "me and Dave made that shit up, but it stood for 'Da Ill Shit, Y'all,' that's what we were using it for."

Rock and Jolicoeur looked for samples that no one else used. Where Marley Marl and MC Shan also checked for distinct samples, including the closing theme of the TV cartoon *The Jetsons* for the song "Jane, Stop This Crazy Thing," even then, the clip was layered atop the same stilted electronic drums that everyone tended to use. Rock and Jolicoeur skipped past James Brown's drummer and opted for psychedelic sounds that evoked space travel. And even if they repurposed an already sampled artist, they made it a point to dig deeper into the lesser-known tracks that other producers might've passed over. The two crafted a song called "Soft Violins," which juxtaposed pounding drums and light keyboard chords. "We would just make quirky stuff," Rock said. "Coming up with stuff was basically a trial-and-error thing, whipping out records and saying, 'Let's take this little piece.' Back then it was a layering style. You could take three different records from three different genres and start making a beat." They focused on creating the strangest instrumentals possible, just to experiment, and the lyrics came only after the sonic foundation was solid: "We were finding anything that could be manipulated and making it sound good."

Mason was a short and stocky DJ and part-time boxer with a laid-back drawl and a big laugh, who relocated to Long Island from Brooklyn in 1984. At just fourteen years old, Mason had already been a working DJ for eight years, cutting his teeth as an apprentice to older players while spinning his own sets in the borough. He DJed a gig at twelve years old in Bushwick, playing a block party at Irving Square Park in 1982. Four years later on Long Island, he scored another opportunity, earning three hundred dollars to spin records at a local function where the noted Queens lyricist Kool G Rap showed up. Because hip-hop was still being erected and rappers weren't ubiquitous, they'd come to events like these to promote themselves. G Rap had just released his first single, the chest-thumping "It's a Demo," and was impressed with the young DJ's skills. "When I saw G Rap at a party I was DJing, I was like, 'I'm on,'" Mason once told Red Bull Music Academy. "He came up to me, said, 'What's up?' I obviously was doing something right." On the weekends, Mason immersed himself in hip-hop and witnessed its composition in the community spaces and backyard parties that became cultural staples. In that way, Mason played a role in the construction of hip-hop, even if history gives rightful deference to bigger names like Kool Herc, Run-D.M.C., and Grandmaster Flash. Though he was just a preteen, Mason was right there in various scenes, quietly making a mark.

An outlandish group like De La needed equally eccentric names. Mercer reversed his DJ moniker, Soundsop, and went by the name Posdnuos (pronounced pasta-noose). The name Soundsop derived from his mother's early years in the 1950s, where "she always would say, 'In my house, you better eat up everything on your plate,' like take that bread and sop up the syrup," Mercer said. "Sound was like I was a DJ, but blending all these sounds and sopping all these sounds. So, when I started back towards trying to be an MC, I just turned everything backwards. 'Sop' became 'Pos' and 'Sound' became 'Dnuos.'" In other moments, he'd call himself Mercenary, Plug Wonder Why, or Plug One, depending on the day. Jolicoeur called himself Plug Two or Trugoy the Dove—"yogurt" spelled backwards—because he just really liked yogurt. "I eat it a lot," he said simply. (Later in his career, he simply went by Dave, which I'll call him in this book.) For his moniker, Mason, or Plug Three, shortened his last name to MASE (Making a Soul Effort) and sometimes went by PA Pasemaster Mase, and later, Maseo, to reflect his title as the band's DJ and coproducer.

In Amityville, Rock introduced Maseo to Pos and Dave with the intent of starting a rap quartet with two DJs and two MCs, a lineup similar to Doug E. Fresh and the Get Fresh Crew or the Ultramagnetic MCs. Initially, though, Maseo wasn't fully invested. He was helping compile a short album for another local rapper named Gangster B called *Cold Waxin' the Party*, an idea conceived by a man named Everett J. Collins Jr., a music teacher who used to write and play drums for the Isley Brothers. The birth of rap spawned a litany of independent record labels, and Collins—perceiving a shifting tide in the industry—had his own imprint and wanted to release Gangster B's music. There was just one problem, though. "It was wack," Maseo once told Red Bull Music Academy. "Really, really wack. Really, really, really wack." Tethered to the project, Maseo, who provided backing vocals and record scratches for it, commiserated with another collaborator who also didn't like the music but felt committed to seeing it through.

"Prince Paul" Huston was something of a celebrity in Amityville, a sixteen-year-old battle DJ and producer who shuttled back and forth to Brooklyn to visit his grandmother and make beats for Stetsasonic, a noted rap collective signed to Tommy Boy Records. Born in Flushing, Queens, Prince Paul moved with his family to Amityville when he was just three years old. The town was sparsely populated in the 1970s, and when Paul's family settled, there were only five houses on the block, a sharp contrast to New York City's density. In the city, he got to work with nascent rappers who saw hip-hop as a way to earn money while expressing themselves. In turn, rappers there were more aggressive than those in the suburbs. On Long Island, they just wanted to be the best in their respective neighborhoods.

Paul represented both sides of the coin: As a producer for Stetsasonic, he was an established entity who showed Long Island natives that they could make it in the music industry. And because he lived in Amityville, Paul had the mental space to create without the external burdens that come naturally from living in New York City. His shot came in 1982, when he was a precocious fifteen-year-old pedaling his bicycle through the neighborhood and some friends and fellow DJs invited him to a local block party where they and others were spinning records. Paul didn't see it as a hangout; he turned it into a battle. He was a showman who'd scratch vinyl under his legs and manipulate the mixer with his mouth. Legend has it he won the battle that day, and his performance caught the attention of Stetsasonic, which had recently won the Mr. Magic Rap Attack competition on 107.5 WBLS. In those days, radio DJs like Magic and Red Alert were the tastemakers; endorsements from them led to record deals, which typically led to fame. Paul produced and DJed for Stetsasonic while he was still in high school. He graduated from Amityville Memorial in 1985.

Maseo and Prince Paul quietly traded notes on the Gangster B project, a Beastie Boys knockoff with reversed drums like their song "Paul Revere"—"in the car, had to be two-three in the morning," Maseo recalled. They both realized it wasn't where they wanted to go creatively. "Me and Mase were sitting there like, 'This is horrible,'" Paul added. "Not necessarily Gangster B's rhyming, but just the concept of biting, 'cause biting was a crime back then." Then, during one of their late-night conversations, Maseo introduced Paul to what was being constructed with De La. "Mase said, 'I got a group, we're called De La Soul,'" Paul remembered. "'I'm gonna come by your house today and bring you a tape.'" How De La came up with the name is a point of contention. If you believe the long-standing narrative, Pos, Dave, and Maseo were sitting around trying to figure out what to call themselves, landing on "From the Soul" until Dave suggested De La ("from the" in Spanish) to throw it off. Daddy-O from Stetsasonic said the name came from their 1986 song "Rock De La Stet." The boys had a meeting at Paul's house, where they played demos and discussed their creative direction. One of the tracks was a rough cut of "Plug Tunin'," a stampeding song with dusty drums, sporadic vocal samples, and muted horn blasts, topped with conversational flows from Pos and Dave. Though the song needed work—"It was dope, but it dragged," Paul recalled—it matched his creative sensibility. "The first thing he said out the gate: 'We can definitely take this to the studio and clean it up,'" Maseo recalled him saying. "I don't know if you're going to get a deal or not, but this is definitely something I'm into creatively." Left alone with the cassette, Paul touched up the beat by adding a Billy Joel sample to entice labels to sign De La.

Despite their potential and Stetsasonic's rising popularity, Paul wasn't enamored of a life in the music business. Unless you were Run--D.M.C. or the Fat Boys, rap just wasn't a thing you could live off of in the mid-'80s, so he worked in the industry and studied audio engineering and business management at Five Towns College in

Seaford. He quickly dropped out. "I would bump heads with the teachers," he said. "It was a horrible experience for me."

Back in Amityville and committed to music full-time, he lived two different lives with Stetsasonic and De La. In Stetsasonic, Paul was the young kid whose ideas weren't always embraced by older group members. In De La, he could fully embrace his quirky side as the elder statesman. There, his propensity to hunt for weird, forgotten audio was met with the same level of enthusiasm. "In De La Soul, I was heard because I was the guy who had already made a record," Paul said. "So they listened to me and listened to everything I said in awe." That brought a power struggle to the newly formed group: with Paul, De La now had a direct line to a possible record deal with Tommy Boy.

Rock, whose brusque demeanor didn't mesh with the group's relaxed manner, was out, even though he helped launch it with Dave and Pos. "I guess I just wasn't the image; I'm a stand-up dude," Rock said. "I'm not gonna go for certain things. I'm not gonna let nobody steer me in the wrong direction. I'm about my business. You're not gonna do nothing crazy and get away with it. So I guess they figured that's a no-no. We had some type of group fallout. A meeting was had without me, and the next thing you know, I was voted out."

Over the years, Pos and Dave have mentioned Rock by name as being the catalyst for the group. Maseo has not. "He became pretty obnoxious, something that didn't fit," he once told Red Bull Music Academy without mentioning Rock by name. "Paul didn't want to work with him either, but when it all came together, he was out the picture."

Rock insisted there were no hard feelings with the group; when their popularity rose, he cheered them along like nothing had changed. But when he heard their eventual debut album, he noticed certain music he worked on being passed off as the new version of De La's. "I'm thinking, 'They're gonna come back and they're not gonna leave me just hanging in the window, regardless of what happened, because we're boys,'" Rock told me. "So then 'Potholes in My Lawn' comes out and I'm like, 'Yo, wait a minute. That's my sample. That's what I was going to use.' Literally left Mase's house, got the record, and brought them the record and made it complete. You can't even give me credit? But then I'm like, 'You know what? Fuck this. If they can do it off some stuff I just started, if I go back and try harder, I can do it, I don't need them.' So that's what I started doing."

His relationship with De La ran hot and cold. Sometimes they'd meet up when the group was back in town; other times, they weren't on speaking terms. Over the years, Rock kept in touch with Pos and Dave, but there was bad blood between him and Maseo until recent years, when their sons encouraged them to bury the hatchet. "I don't have nothing ratchet to say about them," Rock concluded. "We did what we did. I'm glad they did what they did in hip-hop and solidified a spot with something we started out doing as kids in high school. Shit worked, regardless of if I was part of the mainframe. I know I had a great contributing part of what they came to be; I don't care if they deny it or not, but they know Charlie Rock drove what we were riding."

IN ITS NEW FORM, THE MEMBERS OF DE LA SOUL CONVENED AT MASEO'S SPOT, in a nondescript single-family home just a short walk from the high school. They'd pile into a tiny room with production equipment and canary yellow paint covered with scribbled drawings, listening to Paul's advice while searching for new music to manipulate. It was a fluid creative process that took either a few minutes or several hours. Sometimes it was Pos, Dave, or Maseo finding old rock, soul, and funk albums to sample; other times it was Paul who had ideas to run past the fellas. It was a collaborative undertaking. After summer school classes ended late in the morning, around eleven o'clock by Maseo's estimation, the boys started another form of education. "I was in the mix, like, 'No, do it over,'" Paul said. "I used to give them homework sheets every session, like, 'Next session we're coming on Tuesday. Mase, make sure you bring the records such and such. We need verses for this, this, and this.'" The process moved slowly at first. Pos and Dave were still novice rappers, so the idea of performing in front of someone like Prince Paul was slightly intimidating. But he was able to push the guys beyond their comfort zones, taking them to a professional recording studio to compile a demo tape. To pay for the studio, Pos, Dave, and Maseo worked extra shifts—Pos and Dave at Burger King; Maseo at the Wiz record shop. Once in the studio, they worked on the demo overnight for four hours a pop, eventually reshaping "Plug Tunin'" and recording a new song, "Change in Speak."

Rodd Houston, who was an assistant to Silverman, walked into Manhattan's Calliope Studios where Paul and De La were working one night in the summer of 1988. He went in expecting to see Stetsasonic and to chat with group leader Daddy-O but was surprised to see instead the quartet in the booth. Paul was perched behind the studio's production board, and Pos was behind the microphone. The instrumental played. "I remember hearing the first couple of notes of 'Plug Tunin',' and hearing Pos do his first couple of lines," Houston told me. "The cadence, the flow, the rhyme style. It all jumped at me at once. It was so different from what you're used to hearing." Houston sat and listened to the song take shape, then talked to Paul once the group took a break.

"I said, 'You're gonna bring this to Tommy Boy, right?'" he remembered saying. "And Paul was like, 'Fuck Tommy Boy, I'm not fucking with Tommy Boy on this.'"

Stetsasonic didn't like the way their albums were promoted, so Paul couldn't fathom going through that for another project.

Undeterred, Houston tried to convince Paul to play De La's demo for label president Monica Lynch. "In my mind," he said, "this is something I'd like to work with. She would dig it and we'd do a good job marketing it." Though Paul still wasn't swayed after the chat, he wasn't as dead-set against it. Houston was introduced to Pos, Dave, and Maseo; then he left the studio, he said, "humming the melody I heard and thinking, 'Wow, I heard something special.'"

The next day at the office, Houston told Lynch he'd just seen the future. De La Soul was light-years beyond anything he'd heard. Intrigued, she asked Prince Paul to call her and talk about this new group. Before she heard a note, she remembers being impressed with the group's name. It sounded different, intelligent, and creative, and she wanted to hear if the music held up. She pressed play on the orange-labeled cassette and was floored by the muted, dusty sound of "Plug Tunin'," which flew in the face of the big, rock-infused rap that Run-D.M.C., producer Rick Rubin, and Def Jam label head Russell Simmons were pumping out then. That was the sound of New York in the mid-'80s, but by the end of the decade, it had run its course. "Plug Tunin'" was almost understated, a slow-grinding drawl influenced by '60s funk and stoner rock, like some lost missive from a faraway place. De La's image also aligned with what Tommy Boy was selling at the time. The label, in its beginning stages, had found success with the pioneering electro-funk DJ and producer Afrika Bambaataa. Lynch walked the De La tape around the office, playing it for her colleagues. "We were just like, 'Yes. We need to do this,'" she said. "So, I arranged to meet with the group post-haste. I could see they'd appeal to a broader audience right away. There was just something magical about them." The group personified Tommy Boy's mission to be the go-to label for all types of abstract music: "What we've done best has been what we've done with artists who brought something totally new and totally different to the table. In that sense, De La Soul signified a new era at the label."

Despite her enthusiasm, Paul still wasn't keen on having De La sign there. Profile Records, another upstart label, which had Run-D.M.C. on its roster, was offering the group ten thousand dollars just to record a single. Geffen Records offered forty thousand dollars for an album. But after Pos, Dave, and Maseo met with Lynch, they decided to sign with Tommy Boy, because she was so enthralled by the music. Paul wanted De La to sign with Geffen, since they had more cash and promised to put more marketing into the group. But De La wasn't taken by the money or promotional push. They wanted freedom, and Tommy Boy offered that. De La signed with the imprint and were given twenty-five thousand dollars to compile their debut album, *3 Feet High and Rising*, named after the old Johnny Cash song "Five Feet High and Rising." The group contends they received far less than that, something like thirteen thousand dollars total. De La and Tommy Boy would embark on what they thought would be years of trust and goodwill. They soon found out that the music industry doesn't always have your best interests in mind. While record labels can offer financial security you didn't have before, sometimes that security comes with strings. The advances solve short-term challenges like rent, food, and monthly bills, but the artists often wind up in debt to the record labels long-term. Sure, they'll put you in a studio and provide resources for you to make an album, but those costs count against your deal. Then they own your masters and publishing, sometimes in perpetuity. The bulk of the revenue from sales goes to the label first; a fraction—if anything—goes to the artist.

De La Soul created their first album using just two pieces of production equipment, an Eventide harmonizer and a Casio drum machine and sampler, which allowed the group to manipulate sounds in ways that hadn't been done in hip-hop culture. The technology let them rearrange samples to the point where it sounded like a new song. That was the idea, anyway; the music that made its way to *3 Feet High* was largely recognizable. And while this was a De La project, it was very much a collaboration between them and Prince Paul, who carried out many of their ideas and kept refining songs that were still a bit rough sonically, much like he did with "Plug Tunin'." In Calliope Studios, De La tried all sorts of musical tricks, rapping over old instrumentals by Barry White, putting thicker percussion over popular funk breaks, and freestyle-rapping over vocal drums like the rap trio J.J. Fad had done four years prior. "We could put [Hall and Oates singer] Daryl Hall's voice over a Sly and the Family Stone record," Pos once said. "It was amazing." De La didn't waste time compiling music for the album, as they were still riding the creative wave they initiated a short time earlier in Amityville. To those outside their circle, including me, it felt as if De La Soul just sorta blew up overnight, but the ascent from their home studio, to the recording studio, to signing with Tommy Boy and releasing *3 Feet High* was a deliberate process that began in 1987 and ended in 1989.

The excitement spilled over in the studio; the members were nudging each other to even weirder depths. No idea was off the table, even if some of them were abandoned because they didn't fit the scope of the album. An early concept for the backstory involved a make-believe tale of the album's music being transmitted from Mars via three microphone plugs. But the plugs were the actual group members, hence the aliases Plug One, Plug Two, and Plug Three. "It was playful, childlike and fun," Pos said. "We'd rap about 'Mr Fish swimming in a bathroom sink.' We'd dip into psychedelia or jazz. We'd slow down Eddie Murphy's voice and add a car screeching or us yodeling." The song "De La Orgee" came about because the guys were in the booth not knowing what to do and started moaning. Elsewhere, "Take It Off" repurposed the lyrical cadence of the 1987 song "Kick the Ball" by the Philadelphia rap group the Krown Rulers, a De La favorite back then.

The goal, above everything, was to be authentic—and for them, that meant rapping playfully without regard for how the listening public might take it. The objective with anything creative should be to make it for yourself first and let others catch up. And that's what De La did: by sampling genres other producers wouldn't touch, like Hall and Oates and other rock and "blue-eyed soul" that Black people liked but that was still considered white music, De La spoke to groups of listeners that bands not named Run-D.M.C. hadn't yet. That also endeared them to older listeners who listened to contemporary radio and didn't delve too deeply—or at all—into what was happening underground. Doing this pushed De La beyond the parameters of hip-hop into the broader world of pop, making them well known in bigger mainstream circles. Rappers were their heroes, but why not aspire to the same canonical stature as musicians like Stevie Wonder and the Beatles? This type of thinking also epitomized their outside-the-box mentality. From *3 Feet High* moving forward, De La was guided by one question: Why not?

Stevie and the Beatles sourced from various genres, everything from bossa nova to country. The same went for De La during the *3 Feet High* sessions: pulling all this music from new, untapped places ensured the vitality of rap beyond what music purists said about it. Rap was music. It wasn't a fad. There's a science to stitching together old sounds to make something new, and it can be tough to convert listeners who'd rather hear their favorite songs as they were intended. Regardless, when the sheen of this "new thing" wore off, an album like *3 Feet High and Rising* would remain in the lexicon. To De La and Prince Paul, this was high art, and the expression shouldn't be rejected because they were young Black kids articulating themselves in rhythmic verse. "We had something else to say, and we knew there were people out there like us that wanted to hear something else," Dave remembered. "We felt like, if we wanted to look the way we looked and touch on the topics we did, we shouldn't be fearful of doing it just because it was the boasting and the bragging and the gold chain era. We always felt that individualism and creativity and expressing it was most important."

The only rule when creating the album was not to have rules. Forget a plan. Dig for records, come up with the craziest ideas possible, and bring them back to the studio the next day. It's not like Prince Paul was gonna say no to any of it. "Even if he thought what we were doing was stupid or crazy, he didn't tell us," Pos said. "He'd be like, 'Yeah, try it.'" Within these parameters, De La crafted *3 Feet High* in just two months, and it only took that long because Paul was still in Stetsasonic and had to tour in between recording. De La took the train from Long Island to the studio with rough demos of beats, then Paul would touch them up—rinse and repeat.

Fans might have this romanticized vision of Paul and De La working together in the studio, pensive and locked into making what they knew would be a monumental album. But it was the opposite. "We'd just all be sitting around listening to stuff," Paul once said. The studio itself offered a peaceful escape from the hustle of school and the city. Set up like a loft apartment, with a full kitchen and bathroom, it almost didn't feel like they were working. "You could actually look outside and see the landscape of New York City," Pos said. "It was beautiful. There were a lot of creative juices flowing when we were there." The album got done by the artists simply acting silly, by laughing and saying some off-the-wall shit in the microphone booth, each one trying to match the absurdity of the others.

Yet it wasn't entirely spontaneous. While living in the moment was key, Pos, Dave, and Maseo had *3 Feet High* mapped out on paper—everything from what samples Maseo should scratch to what voices to add to the songs—then they'd deviate from the plan if they saw a friend in another recording session. Contemporaries like MC Lyte and Q-Tip were simply background voices, making *3 Feet High* a fully communal effort without egos. That's mostly because they didn't know what they were doing. In hindsight, it's wild to think that eventual legends like Lyte and Tip were plus-ones in any capacity, but it speaks to the unknown that rap was at the time, before self-pride got in the way of community. De La's "anything goes" style was powered by a wandering ethos that somehow landed in outer space. Between their dusty drums and obscure vocal samples, it felt distant yet alluring, a new masterpiece from a bygone era of Black experimentation. It was Melvin Van Peebles meets Bootsy Collins, Jimi Hendrix, and Rotary Connection. From the beginning, the trio rebuked any classification that tethered their sound to rap alone; instead, De La was just De La, the friendly avant-garde trio with a golden ear for unconventional themes and concepts.

Though I was just eight years old in 1989, my identity was already coming through. I was an old soul who appreciated the likes of Van Peebles and Bootsy, even if rap was more compatible. I grew up with aunts who played psychedelic rock and pop, a mother who liked everything from Madonna to Al Green, and a grandmother who played traditional gospel around the house. My cousin jokes that I've been studying my craft since I was two or three; he says all you had to do was sit me in front of MTV and I wouldn't bother anyone the whole day. Despite my age, I was already deeply immersed in music and hip-hop culture, even if I didn't fully understand its importance. The music felt fresh and inspirational, tailored to kids and young adults. R&B and gospel were reserved for the older folks in the family, and funk—*well*—that was reserved for my free-spirited aunts Pam, Claudia, and Claudette. I came of age as rap came of age, when groups like Public Enemy and Boogie Down Productions were releasing their first albums. I was listening to all kinds of rap records that I was too young to be hearing. My family was liberal in that way, though: there weren't many restrictions on entertainment (except *Eddie Murphy Raw*; we were banned from watching that), and my mom would take me to the record store to buy any album within reason: Prince's *Lovesexy* (despite the cover art), Public Enemy's *Fear of a Black Planet*, D-Nice's *Call Me D-Nice*.

While I don't remember buying De La Soul's *3 Feet High and Rising*, I do remember it being part of the household. Maybe it was my cousin Eric's copy. Or somebody else's. That I can't remember just how the album got there speaks to the ubiquity of De La as a whole. They've always been there just because. The first time I played it was in my aunt Pam's townhome. They seemed innocent, and the music bore that out, despite the sometimes juvenile nature of the proceedings. It just didn't seem like these dudes could have legitimate beef with anyone.

TOMMY BOY AND DE LA HAD A COMPLICATED RELATIONSHIP, AS IS COMMON with artists focused on making music and not the commercial side of it. Even the cover art for *3 Feet High* led to contention. Label president Lynch reportedly came up with the idea to make the group look like a unit from the '60s, which De La didn't like but went along with anyway. Despite their apprehension, the cover—a bright yellow sleeve with orange and blue flowers (a nod to the New York Knicks?) and pink and green lettering—and the album marketing made them stand out, which helped the group become who they are. So, as easy as it is to blame Tommy Boy for the financial setbacks following *3 Feet High and Rising*'s release, they should also be commended for their marketing prowess. While they couldn't know the impact their ideas would make, they thought outside the box, enticing other labels to do the same.

From the music to the physical packaging, De La was heavily influenced by George Clinton and Parliament-Funkadelic, even down to the cartoons drawn in the liner notes and the backstory of the LP. Pos, in particular, was inspired by the narratives Clinton used to attach to his albums and wanted *3 Feet High* to have the same essence: free, perplexing, and weird, the type of music you're drawn to but can't quite articulate why.

It was released just four days before another worldwide phenomenon hit shelves: *Girl You Know It's True* by the German R&B duo Milli Vanilli, a superstar act that rose to prominence behind the title track and the song "Blame It on the Rain" but had their Grammy Award stripped after it was revealed that they didn't actually sing the songs on their LP. Conversely, *3 Feet High* was a slow-moving locomotive gathering steam with the rap heads. The first four singles catered specifically to that sect; "Me Myself and I" became a number one song that propelled the album to gold and platinum sales. For the guys themselves, the release came with a sense of excitement, relief, and disbelief, much like for anyone putting out something creative for public consumption. By the time it's in stores, it's been scrutinized and reworked so many times that it's a miracle the project still exists. *3 Feet High* felt like a culmination and a launching pad, a chance for them to breathe while bracing for the unknown. Pos, Dave, and Maseo couldn't believe they had a rap album in the world, and one that listeners actually liked. There was shock, but also accomplishment.

Critically, music journalists used all the adjectives to assess the LP. "Nothing if not zany," the writer Michael Azerrad penned in the March 23, 1989, issue of *Rolling Stone*. "One of the most original rap records ever to come down the pike, the inventive, playful *3 Feet High and Rising* stands staid rap conventions on their def ear." Calling their music "maddeningly disjunct," *Village Voice* critic Robert Christgau said the album was "radically unlike any rap you or anybody else has ever heard." These assessments were received and appreciated, but the greatest compliments came from their peers. "*3 Feet High and Rising* also sounded like those tapes you made when you were a little kid, on your tape deck," Ad-Rock of Beastie Boys declared.

Thirty years later, it's tough to say whether or not they achieved the goal—even the staunchest De La fans admit the album took some getting used to—but you don't become a legend by being basic. Without their fearlessness, they don't craft interludes like "Can U Keep a Secret" and "I Can Do Anything (Delacratic)," the former a whispery comedic shout to Silly Putty and haircuts over a West African funk drum loop, the latter a vocal parody with copious amounts of beatboxing. Rappers took themselves seriously (perhaps too seriously) in the '80s, and compared with their peers, parts of *3 Feet High* were downright sophomoric and worthy of ridicule. On "Take It Off," De La wagged a finger at everything that constituted hip-hop culture: durags, shell-toe Adidas with fat laces, Jheri curls, and bomber jackets. Though they didn't mention them by name, they were dissing the likes of Run-D.M.C. and N.W.A, acts who fit the profile of what was thought to be typical. Surely they were having fun, but De La sometimes came off as pretentious and self-righteous. Who were they to disparage the way others expressed creativity when they weren't typical themselves? Then there was the song "Tread Water," a nursery rhyme set in a pond and featuring rhymes about crocodiles and squirrels; it was corny and hasn't aged well. "I never really liked that record," Pos once said. "We actually sat down in Paul's room and came up with that idea," Dave continued. "The sample just sounded so happy-go-lucky, skipping, playing hopscotch, the whole walking through the water and meeting animals and crocodiles and telling a story. . . . Paul was always instigating our foolishness. When we started talking about meeting Mr. Crocodile, his eyes just lit up. He was like, 'Yeah, you talk about Mr. Crocodile, and you talk about meeting Mr. Rabbit.' So blame that one on Paul." Examples like that showed that De La needed accountability. Not every idea was a good one.

Touré Neblett, the noted music journalist and author, bought *3 Feet High* on cassette based on the strength of "Me Myself and

I," the second-to-last track recorded for the LP, which was added because the label needed a single with broader appeal. Neblett, who grew up in the Boston area, fit squarely within De La's demographic: he liked all kinds of music, adored the Beatles, and played tennis in his spare time. While these affinities aren't especially frowned upon in the Black community, they are thought to be white activities that somehow diminish your Blackness if you're into them. "I knew who I was, but I also knew I was a little different," Neblett once wrote in a June 14, 2018, essay in the *Guardian*. "The icons of blackness then were hyper black. . . . Their performance of blackness was far from mine." Listening to the album in his old Honda Prelude, he ejected it from the deck and threw it in the backseat in disgust, thinking it was nonsense at certain spots. Then he heard "Potholes in My Lawn," a sly diss track about those who mimic their beats and rhythmic cadences, on the radio and fished the tape from the backseat. "They had an expansive view of what hip-hop could be," Neblett told me. "It could be noisy, it could be all these different things. It didn't have to be so braggadocious. When I heard De La, I felt more pulled into hip-hop than I did before. They showed that hip-hop can be about silliness without being silly."

Goofy moments were met with just as many serious ones that chronicled the perils of their neighborhood and inner cities across America. On the song "Ghetto Thang," Pos rapped about a fourteen-year-old mother raising twins and how society disregarded her and others who weren't wealthy. "Negative's the attitude that runs the show," he reflected, "when the stage is the G-H-E-T-T-O." In his verse, Dave dipped into broader societal decay, offering quick thoughts about the root causes of inner-city despair that produced someone like the fourteen-year-old: the alcoholism that stemmed from the widespread dearth of opportunities, even the housing projects that encased the struggle. So when he said "Infested are the halls, also the brains / Daddy's broken down from ghetto pains," Dave indicted the local, state, and federal governments that allowed poverty to fester in such places. Then there was "Say No Go," which spoke directly to the crack cocaine epidemic ravaging Black communities throughout the country. Though they didn't partake in the game themselves, De La knew drug dealers and sometimes congregated on corners where crime was an issue.

Rap hadn't glamorized drug dealing just yet; that would occur in the next decade. By the late '80s, songs like "Self Destruction," helmed by Boogie Down Productions and featuring everyone from MC Lyte and Kool Moe Dee to Heavy D, Public Enemy, and Stetsasonic, were aimed at stopping drug use in Black communities and the subsequent violent crime that arose. "Say No Go" played into the "Just Say No" ad campaign, a slogan instituted by first lady Nancy Reagan as part of the Reagan administration's so-called War on Drugs, which disproportionately targeted Black people and put low-level offenders in prison for long stints. Whites arrested for the same offenses were given lesser jail time. Decades after the crack era subsided, local officials still struggled to revamp the corner of Albany and Great Neck, and there remains a wide chasm between advantaged and economically disadvantaged populations.

Young women, like the one Pos rapped about on "Ghetto Thang," are still ignored, denied the grace and resources they need to thrive. While *3 Feet High* wasn't meant to solve the world's ills, it shed light on systemic challenges with the same earnestness as serious-minded rappers like Chuck D and KRS-One. But where Chuck spoke with a furrowed brow and KRS with occasionally preachy finger-pointing, De La took a yeoman's approach to rap, speaking to their listeners as equals. Sure, you were going to learn about racism and socioeconomic disparities through Chuck's and KRS's work, but De La rapped about these things lightheartedly (at least at first). Their music felt like an intimate conversation, and the group spoke for those who wanted change without having to shout their demands through a bullhorn.

De La wanted to call for the same progress, but with a softer touch that could reach more ears. That cut both ways for the group: On one end, *3 Feet High* was embraced for speaking to a section of Blackness that had been ignored to that point. But it also catered to white consumers and the critical establishment that fetishized the spoils of hip-hop culture while sidestepping the struggles of Black people. Some saw De La as the rap you played for those who weren't really into the genre. There was the false notion that they were too palatable to those who didn't share their skin color. It wasn't gritty or Black enough for the heads who saw rap as an exclusive genre for their voices alone.

Beastie Boys—the trio of Adam Yauch, Mike D, and Ad-Rock, whose music spanned punk and rap—released *Paul's Boutique* in the summer of 1989, three months after *3 Feet High* and a year after Public Enemy's 1988 record *It Takes a Nation of Millions to Hold Us Back*. Though *Boutique* would become a go-to album in the Beasties' discography, it initially got swamped by the tidal wave of those two albums. "We put every idea that we had into that record, every sample, everything that we thought was funny to each other," Mike D said in 2020. "It's like that thing where you work really hard on a record and you think it's dope, and we put it out and it's crickets." Make no mistake, they adored the De La and Public Enemy albums, but to be ignored in the wake of *3 Feet High* and *Nation of Millions* left a sour taste. There was "this moment where you love these records so much and you're thrilled and you love them and you're completely defeated at the same time," Mike added.

This was the impact of *3 Feet High*—sudden and unexpected, an album you couldn't quite fathom with a sound you couldn't place. For acts like Beastie Boys, whose outsider aura mirrored De La's, it was challenging to operate in the same space, to mix genres and sampling with the same kaleidoscopic verve and still not hit the mark. Others overthought what seemed natural for De La; years later, critics, musicians, and listeners are still trying to make sense of—and mimic—the album's broad sonic mosaic. De La themselves have a complicated relationship with the album: On one end, it harbored the most creative freedom and best represented what could have been for the group. It was the most innocent, the most optimistic, the most carefree. It was also the beginning of a very slow descent. Right away, the band soured on the music business and took issue with the branding of their sound. The disillusion only got worse over time.

OTHERS FROM THE BROTHER PLANET

THOUGH DE LA SOUL WAS GENERATING A BUZZ IN 1989, THEIR PEERS still didn't know what to make of them. Their first performance took place in Union Square, a grungy section of downtown Manhattan full of hollowed-out warehouses and illegal nightclubs that became the core of countercultural movements like hip-hop and punk. It was fertile ground for disillusioned kids looking to create their own utopia. It made sense for De La to be there: their music, which spoke to everyone but didn't fit in anywhere, was fussy and agitated like the Ramones and Talking Heads, both of whom got their start in the same part of town. Rap also fit the ethos, and though it was birthed some twelve miles north in the Bronx, it made an impact just like the other work being trumpeted in spots like CBGB, where acts like the Dead Boys and Joan Jett spawned the first iterations of new wave and grunge.

Hip-hop wasn't just growing in the city; it was catching on nationally, its stars commingling in wider pop culture, starring in films and playing big arenas throughout the country. Looking back, it was arguably the golden era, a time when creativity was just as valued as the bottom line, and rappers could draw crowds and still be bizarre as hell. While such distinctiveness was embraced throughout the city, a monthly event paved the way for all sorts of outcasts to convene and be showcased.

Patrick Moxey was a twenty-four-year-old promoter who used to book groups like Beastie Boys for his warehouse parties in old olive oil factories and housing centers for El Salvadoran refugees. He'd scrape together a few dollars, buy massive sound systems, and cohost the shows with his friend Chuck Crook, a South Carolina–born promoter who brought flavor to the events by setting up juice bars and skateboard ramps in the event space. Along with De La, the parties helped launch the careers of A Tribe Called Quest and Black Sheep and became a staple for those looking to blow off steam from the workweek. From Thursday to Saturday, the parties—each one named after a candy bar and centering on a different musical genre—showcased DJs like Kid Capri and Clark Kent and were a melting pot for future stars and others doing cool things across mediums. The film director Spike Lee would show up, as would the jazz saxophonist Branford Marsalis, who, along with his younger brother Wynton, led the way for jazz music's resurgence in the 1980s. Q-Tip would occasionally spin records. "It was such a cultural time, just an incredible time in music," Moxey told me. "Our friends were photographers, stylists, or rappers. We wouldn't let anyone in with a suit and tie." Because they were illegal venues, Moxey had to keep moving where the events happened. Patrons had to call his answering machine (if you had the number) and get the address to even know where the parties were being held from week to week.

When De La played his Payday party in 1988, "Potholes in My Lawn" had been released as the second single from *3 Feet High and Rising*, and some wondered how these kids would fare in a place known for having rough clientele. Dante Ross, an A&R who was assigned to De La as an employee at Tommy Boy Records, remembered pressure on the group to perform live, given the sudden buzz around them. But they had never played a show, and there was concern that the gig wouldn't live up to the music. Before the show, the label booked the Rocket Rehearsal Studio on West Thirtieth Street for De La to iron out their set. Backup dancers held up large cue cards with the lyrics scribbled on them, and De La—along with their friend Gran-E— performed coordinated dance moves that matched what was being shown on the card. "It was cool, pretty funny, and original, just like the music, and I thought it had a chance to make people notice," Ross recalled.

At the gig, the band diffused all tension. Pos and Dave wore matching baggy tan checkered pants and jet-black button-down dress shirts, while Maseo donned a white shirt and gold chain with a big red and white clock dangling from his neck. "De La was throwing flowers at the audience," Moxey said. "I was like, 'Are these guys gonna get shot?'" Their positivity disarmed the crowd and garnered respect; De La wasn't like anything they'd seen before. "People loved the show, even the most hardcore people," Moxey recalled. "Everybody realized this was something different."

Stetsasonic was set to headline De La's gig, but the drama with the label boiled over to the point where Stetsasonic, citing troubles with the venue's sound, decided not to perform, leaving De La in the lurch. Without the draw of Stetsasonic, there was no reason for peers and industry types to check out an inexperienced band like theirs. Surprisingly, though, the heavy hitters showed up—Lyor Cohen,

Russell Simmons, Cory Robbins, and Fab 5 Freddy—and somewhere around one in the morning, De La was introduced by their dancers and Gran-E with a dance interpretation of the album track "Change in Speak." They rapped some of it before delving into "Plug Tunin'" and winning over the crowd. "By the start of the second verse," Ross added, "the house was rapping along with the cue cards, more or less, and I knew right then and there that these guys had something really special." Everyone wanted a piece of De La; the rapper D.M.C. even asked the group to get back onstage and perform the same set again. It was that dope.

The gig went well enough, but they needed to strengthen their live show to hang with the LLs and Rakims. Performing a handful of songs with two dancers and a few cue cards wouldn't land as well in an arena full of people who weren't there for them. "We heard the talking and we had to suck it up and get our show right," Pos once told Ross. "We didn't really have a choice, to be honest." The live show alone can make or break any artist. If you rock the crowd, you can sustain yourself on the road. If your recorded sound is solid but not your live show, you can still earn a living, though you're somewhat limited in the amount of money you can bring in. It's no secret that tour money is the best money. Albums are good for the marketplace, but those sales benefit labels before artists.

The group faced a challenge: with all the sampling and coded language in their music, it could be tough to comprehend, and it was challenging to present both aspects in a carefully constructed set. The muted drums and frizzy samples on their studio albums didn't sound good in cavernous venues; instead, it sounded like a jumbled mass tumbling from the speakers. Just two months after their debut album was released, they opened for the rock band Living Colour at the Ritz in Manhattan's East Village neighborhood. The show was messy and only got better when Pos and Dave started rhyming in unison and bantering with each other onstage. That it felt like practice on Long Island made the show feel more authentic than what they had been doing. "At their best they seemed on the verge of inventing a new type of concert," the music critic Peter Watrous wrote in a June 27, 1989, review, "The Uncluttered Hip-Hop of De La Soul," in the *New York Times*. "Part talk show, part rap concert—where their funny conversations and routines were as important as their raps." Watrous was onto something: De La worked best when they were having fun, cracking jokes on each other or sticking it to their common enemy—the music industry. When it felt like they were rapping without a crowd, you got to see what it was like in the suburbs, a year before fame was tangible. De La shone best when it seemed we were eavesdropping on inside jokes and other material we weren't supposed to hear.

They wouldn't have improved their show without Asia Minor, a sixteen-year-old dancer who met Pos under dubious circumstances. It was two in the morning on a Thursday night, and she'd been kicked out of her home by a mother who was hooked on drugs. At the behest of her brother, she went downtown and bumped into a group of girls from the Smith Projects, who took her to the first ever Zulu Nation party at Hotel Amazon. De La, Big Daddy Kane, Rakim, Nice & Smooth, and an unknown rapper named Guru all performed. "I was freshly traumatized, so I had no time to think and had to enjoy the moment," Minor told me. She started dancing and felt a tap on her shoulder; it was Pos. "He was like, 'Yo, your moves are really dope! I'd love for you to dance with us.'" She shrugged him off and kept dancing, doing her best to survive the night. Plus she didn't know who Pos was or what De La represented. To her, he was just some dude who maybe didn't have good intentions.

Two months later, she was dancing at another club when she felt another tap on her shoulder. Pos's brother Lucky (the spitting image of Pos) pleaded with Minor to call the De La Soul member to discuss the possibility of dancing with the group. She still remembers Mercer's phone number: "It was one eight-hundred four nine five Plug One." At the time, Minor was homeless while attending school, working odd jobs, going to nightclubs, and finding somewhere to crash at night. She was a young girl in 1980s New York City, so she was naturally skeptical of a rapper asking her to hit the road with his band for months at a time. Yet she trusted Pos enough to give De La a shot. He seemed sincere. The opportunity proved beneficial to both. The band got someone to strengthen their live show, and Minor proved she could choreograph a large-scale concert with one of hip-hop's emerging talents, even though she was underage. "They could have gotten in trouble legally; there weren't Amber Alerts out on me back then," Minor reflected. "I could have been a liability, you know? I've never had an opportunity like that handed to me. It was life-changing."

Four months after *3 Feet High*'s release, De La went on their first tour, with Big Daddy Kane, Slick Rick, LL Cool J, and EPMD, a monthlong jaunt sponsored by Rush Artist Management that included stops in Philadelphia and Cincinnati and presented another challenge for the Long Island group: because they rapped about such disparate topics as aquatic life and outer space, certain fans didn't know what to expect. Rappers assumed De La would roll over because they didn't look intimidating, but folks learned the hard way that they weren't pushovers. With every fight on the road, "I'd be like, 'Yo, did this really happen?,'" thinking it's just rumors," Prince Paul recalled. "And they'd go, 'Yeah, we shot up the car. Yeah, we beat up that guy.'" But it wasn't just random folks and other rappers who tested the group; label executives also thought they could take advantage of De La financially. "They wanted to test them Long Island kids who had flowers in their pictures," Dave told *Mass Appeal* for their 2016 documentary *De La Soul Is Not Dead*. It's no wonder they soured on the business. They didn't have the space to grow in their own way as young Black men. De La wasn't being marketed just to Black audiences; they were being packaged as safe. There was one tour poster in particular in which a white guy in a tweed suit is seen standing with a vinyl copy of *3 Feet High and Rising*. The caption: "I Came in for U2, I Came out with De La Soul."

Of course there was room for variation—Black people didn't want to fight the power all the time—but De La was carefree: no less aware of Reaganomics, poverty, and the crack cocaine epidemic, but a friendlier alternative. Silverman has said that more white people started rapping because of *3 Feet High and Rising*, and that the LP was more influential for whites than other records. He's also called it the Monty Python of hip-hop, comparing it to the irreverent British sketch comedy show with all its goofy premises and deep laugh-out-loud moments. While Silverman's praise was meant as a compliment, it also resurfaced a problem that tends to occur when white people discuss Black art. There's a tendency to compare it to something of their own culture. Black music can't just exist on its own; there has to be an entry point, some sort of comparison to white culture to validate its existence.

Now back to that tour poster: At the bottom is a quote from a *Los Angeles Times* album review calling *3 Feet High* "The Sergeant Peppers' [*sic*] of the Eighties," referring to the Beatles' 1967 LP *Sgt. Pepper's Lonely Hearts Club Band*, which, through unique sonic engineering from producer George Martin, shifted the sound of rock music. After *Sgt. Pepper's*, it wasn't odd to hear the drums way back in the left channel, or the vocals pitched to the right just a bit. Not only was that comparison a gross overreaction to De La's debut, but it forced them into a box that didn't fit. It also set the bar so high that no matter what they released next, the summit of *3 Feet High* would be impossible to top. Nonetheless, the album made a global impact, and Minor remembered a clear distinction before and after the release of "Potholes in My Lawn" as a single. Before its unveiling, the crowd's response to De La was fine; after it, fans everywhere—from

Australia, to Amsterdam, to the United Kingdom—knew the ins and outs of *3 Feet High*—the skits, song lyrics, everything. "When we did Wembley Stadium in London, it was the most shocking thing I'd ever seen in my life," she told me. "It was a mass of people on people. And mind you, we were like the only rap group besides Public Enemy that was touring Europe, because De La broke on the pop side earlier than everybody else."

Creatively, De La were descendants of Jungle Brothers, a trio that made a blueprint for the wave of Black liberation rap that swept through the genre in the late '80s and early '90s. But before they released their debut album, *Straight out the Jungle*, in 1988 (less than a year before *3 Feet High and Rising*), Bam, Sammy B, and Mike G were three school-aged students who met in Harlem in 1985. Without the JBs' formation and willingness to be peculiar, there's no path for De La to follow. Much like their successors, Jungle Brothers met through a shared love of hip-hop. They played talent shows throughout the city and refined their sound through underground mixtapes. Local radio took interest, which raised the band's profile and led to wider interest from listeners. In those days, it was harder to stand out. Hip-hop was a lot less crowded, and, well, you actually had to be intriguing and different to get anyone's attention. That's not to say there aren't great rappers today. I'm not some older dude yelling at a cloud. But it wasn't like it is today, where anyone with a Wi-Fi connection can upload music to a streaming platform and hope for the best. Back then, groups like Jungle Brothers and De La had to take incremental steps toward their dreams. "It wasn't like everybody could do it," Mike G said, side-eyeing today's industry. "There weren't that many artists, but everyone came with something different. You either came original or you didn't come at all."

If you were wack, your peers would let you know. You'd either get clowned openly, beaten up, or thrown off the stage. If you were dope, though, chances were you had something exceptional. Such was the case for Jungle Brothers and their debut album, which stood out due to its assortment of drum breaks that evoked an era just before them, when polyrhythmic funk, spoken-word poetry, and avant-garde jazz samples from underground labels like Strata-East and Flying Dutchman signaled a new awakening in Black American communities. Their lyrical approach was linear: the JBs created a counterbalance within their music, speaking the same sort of Black pride as James Brown or Sly and the Family Stone. The JBs spoke to the children of the pro-Black era, resurrecting the brassy soul they heard on scratchy vinyl as kids. "We didn't want to create some type of character that was out of reach," Mike G told me. "I felt like whoever I was on the mic I had to be in real life. I didn't want to create some big persona. I wanted to keep it real and uplift the people . . . that common-man vibe, that people's-people kind of deal. We wanted to turn our concrete jungle into something more grand, mystical, and lovely." That describes De La Soul too. But where Jungle Brothers are still vastly underrated in the pantheon of rap greats, De La made such an impact that they're still held captive by the music they made as teenagers. It's a good challenge to have—Who doesn't want to be celebrated?—but it's tough when your evolution is tied to something you created years ago.

The JBs came across De La like everyone else did, through the trio's debut song "Plug Tunin'," which caught fire shortly after *Straight out the Jungle* was released. "That thing hit the ground running," Mike G remembered. "That thing resonated, man." Because of the group's name, the JBs' Afrika Baby Bam thought De La Soul was a Hispanic rap group. "There's no video, no promo pictures," Maseo remembered. "Everybody thought we were Puerto Rican." Naturally, listeners and critics lumped De La and Jungle Brothers together as the torchbearers of a new wave of psychedelic Afrocentricity in rap music, where groups like them prioritized substance over style without sacrificing swag. Their crews were cool, too: not unattainable, just seemingly regular guys who could rhyme. In 1989, during a one-off show in Boston, the groups bonded over a shared admiration of each other's clothing and thought to strike up a conversation. But then a fight broke out elsewhere, causing everyone to scatter. Amid the chaos, De La and Jungle Brothers swapped pleasantries and vowed to catch up later.

Bam noticed striking similarities between them and De La. It was as if they spoke the same dialect, like they were of the same tribe. Back in New York, the two groups bumped into each other at clubs throughout the city.

They also started running around with a young upstart band named A Tribe Called Quest. They'd call themselves the Native Tongues, a crew of like-minded lyricists who brought Afrocentricity to hip-hop. Much like the jazz pianist Sun Ra wore Egyptian finery and discussed Black freedom through his music, the Native Tongues showed rappers that love and companionship don't make you weak. In fact, it was OK to be gentle, to hug people, to smile and have fun. As a child, I'm taking in these positive images and wondering how this can be. I'm not just blown away by the notion of rappers being outwardly affectionate; I can't believe I'm seeing people on TV so close to my own personal aesthetic.

I've always thought the Native Tongues' formation was some magnificent story, but it wasn't. There was no grand meeting of the minds, no roundtable chats about starting a collective. Instead, the crew that would come to influence generations of socially conscious rappers came together as friends who liked the same music and attended each other's studio sessions. Bam would call Pos, De La Soul's de facto leader, to talk about the music they were making.

Concurrently, Q-Tip, Jarobi, Ali Shaheed Muhammad, and Phife Dawg were building the foundation for Tribe. Around this time, in 1988, Jungle Brothers were headed overseas on an extensive tour to promote their album. By the time they returned, De La was working on a massive posse cut called "Buddy," which would appear near the end of *3 Feet High and Rising*. The beat sampled an old song by the Commodores titled "Girl, I Think the World About You," which Maseo would play in the studio even as the group worked on other tracks. "Buddy" itself was recorded under tenuous circumstances, with the deadline looming for De La to submit the album and just about a week to record the song. Q-Tip and Jungle Brothers went to the studio session. De La asked their new friends if they wanted to spit some verses on it. They agreed.

Neither Jungle Brothers nor De La knew it then, but the track would define the collective. Featuring verses from the JBs, a young British rapper named Monie Love, the upstart New Jersey rapper Queen Latifah, and Q-Tip from Tribe (Phife's verse was cut), "Buddy" crystallized the Native Tongues as a bona fide force. Their unification sent a strong message to braggadocious MCs that a new crew was coming.

But once the excitement of *3 Feet High* began to wear off, the members of De La Soul regrouped as best as they could, stepping out of the spotlight for a brief second, knowing there'd be external pressure to top what they'd done already. At this point in their career—just one year in, mind you—the band was stuck. If they walked away, they risked losing the global audience they worked hard to amass. If they continued, they'd likely have to bend somewhat to the will of Tommy Boy executives and industry bureaucracy. They'd hang around, sure; to be a teenage rap star was still the ultimate allure. Yet somehow, someway, they needed to unload the bullshit. The music was the best way to do so.

OFF THE ROAD AND BACK IN NEW YORK CITY, POS, DAVE, AND MASEO WERE
exhausted. It was the longest they'd stayed away from home, and the
wear and tear of performing in foreign spaces had taken a toll. The
band was also growing frustrated because they no longer had time
to do the one thing they wanted to do: create. The idea of De La
Soul had swelled beyond the music, and there was concern they were
losing control of their schedules along with the sense of why they got
into music in the first place. To Pos, Dave, and Maseo, they were just
regular guys expressing themselves, but to listeners, they were giants.
It created strain. Despite their fatigue, the bigwigs at Tommy Boy
wanted De La to build upon the success of *3 Feet High and Rising*
with a new album that mimicked the first one, and the group's new
management, Rush Artist Management, initiated an intense press
schedule that kept them away from the recording studio.

One day during a meeting, the group noticed a large whiteboard
with the itineraries of other big-name artists on the roster. Dave, in
a moment of good-natured protest, went up and erased all of De La's
dates and wrote five words that would become a rallying cry for the
group's mental health and the tone of their music going forward: "De
La Soul is dead"—as in physically tired and not liking how they were
pigeonholed. "We all started dying laughing," Pos said of the joke.
"You know, like, he was just tired of it, 'Yo, I wanna stay home. I
don't want to go out on the road.' In that very moment, it resonated
with us like, 'This could be a dope album title.' Then it all started
from there."

De La didn't mimic *3 Feet High and Rising*; they mocked it with a
storyline centered on schoolchildren who find the group's cassette in a
trash can. Compared with the jovial nature of *3 Feet High*, *De La Soul
Is Dead*, released in May 1991, was a bleak and acerbic response to
the industry and the band's mounting frustrations, a kiss-off to those

who had crossed them over the previous three years. Where the focus of the first album was to have fun as babies in the music business, *De La Soul Is Dead* found the group taking stock of what they'd seen and not liking the view. And where the first record sought to present De La as one voice, the sophomore album was built to allow Pos, Dave, and Maseo to shine individually. The group wasn't in the mood for jokes; they, and rap music as a whole, had grown incredibly dark and uncertain.

A CLASSIC FOUND IN THE GARBAGE

BY 1990, HIP-HOP WAS BEING ACCEPTED WITHIN BROADER POP culture. No longer was it a small conversation between those who helped build it; rather, it was now being commodified and used in films and commercials to sell sneakers and soda. There was still this feeling that rappers were *those people over there*, not serious musicians to be respected. Mainstream rap was beginning to sound watered down. Certain rappers responded.

The easiest targets were MC Hammer and Vanilla Ice, both of whom found success by mixing rap and pop music, which made for a more festive style that rankled rap purists. The two drew ire from De La Soul and A Tribe Called Quest, both of whom blamed

Hammer and Ice for what was wrong in the genre. As they saw it, hip-hop remained the voice of underserved Black and brown kids, and to synthesize it with pop music—a genre typically reserved for white performers—diluted the message and the intent. Like-minded rappers took not-so-subtle shots at the two: on its song "Pop Goes the Weasel," 3rd Bass, a noted interracial rap trio signed to Def Jam, called Ice a "phony entertainer" and a corporate shill.

Hammer, with his repurposed up-tempo funk dance beats, was attacked by groups like Tribe, 3rd Bass, and De La for making certain strains of Black music sound too sterile. As they saw it, rap was supposed to sound dirty, or at least have some heart. They didn't think that Hammer, with his shoulder pads and parachute pants, represented Blackness. The thought was he, like Ice, catered to those who knew nothing about hip-hop culture. They were taken to task on *De La Soul Is Dead*, *3 Feet High*'s sardonic successor.

Their displeasure with everything came out through the samples they chose and the tempos they slowed to a wobble. It embodied how they were feeling. "As we're recording the album, I remember telling the guys, 'This is a very mean record, this is a clear departure,'" Prince Paul said. "They're beating people up. They're addressing every possible thing that annoys them." They also approached their sophomore LP with a bit of resignation: On the first record, De La didn't adhere to what they were supposed to be. Yet the press still derided them with nods to flowers and hippy culture. So *De La Soul Is Dead* was more of a "Fuck it, let's keep doing us" record. "It's all about dying and being rejuvenated as something else," Pos once said. "Whatever they name us they're gonna name us." *De La Soul Is Dead* was the group's attempt to grow from naive teens to experienced young adults—Dave was twenty-two; Pos and Maseo were twenty-one—not unlike pop boy bands moving from sweet bops to adult fare.

They didn't waste time delving into the fray: The album opens with a schoolyard conversation in which a group of young girls talk about Vanilla Ice's body while a kid named Jeff finds a De La Soul cassette in the garbage. He is clowned for having gums like Arsenio Hall, letting the late-night host know they hadn't forgotten about his subtle diss. And that is just the intro. Elsewhere on the album, De La discussed crack cocaine and domestic abuse, more serious themes for what had been considered a playful group. There is a song like "Pease Porridge," where the group addressed their public image and the tussles they got into on the road. In his verse, Pos spoke to the contrast of fame and chicanery that came to dot De La's existence. Here, he's the successful musician with hit records on the radio who still has love from local neighborhoods. The "Pease Porridge" refers to the peace they proclaimed on the first album; now, in the early '90s, "loonies [were] acting real bold." The track jokingly advises against that, as if to say "Just because we have wild hairstyles and wear medallions and baggy clothes, don't think we can't put hands on you." With success came resentment, then the boxes in which critics wanted to fit the group. The notion that they could commit violence was stunning to folks. Sometimes they had to protect themselves from rabid fans too.

Aspiring rappers would run up on Prince Paul with demo tapes, and De La themselves had groupies. They couldn't just walk down the street; they had to run into clothing stores and hide until the coast was clear. As weird as this notoriety was for De La, they low-key (or perhaps high-key) loved being rap stars. Some of this newfound ego made its way into the music, and parts of *De La Soul Is Dead* were more pretentious than *3 Feet High*'s more goofy moments, which alienated parts of their fan base while delighting others. Personally, I didn't fall in love with *De La Soul Is Dead* right away. I was expecting *3 Feet High and Rising 2*, not realizing there was no way to capture the magic of that album twice. I was in the fifth grade and didn't know any better, and just wanted my favorite group to make the same record over and over again. It wasn't until I got older that I realized that such thinking was wrongheaded. Artists are supposed to evolve and bring listeners with them. My wanting them to stay the same was selfish.

De La exuded the same sort of braggadocio their peers did, though in their case, the bragging chided girls who dissed them and naysayers who thought they were weird. Compared with *3 Feet High*'s kitchen sink ethos, *De La Soul Is Dead* was a "told you so" record on which the band, to a certain extent, talked shit about everyone they could, spraying bullets and sorting out the bodies later. And it was much more than just an outward-facing assessment of national carnage. On the song "My Brother's a Basehead," Pos chided his brother, spinning a visceral tale of drug abuse that put a strain on the family and fractured their relationship. Pos and his brother Tyrone had been especially close, but just like thousands of others during the crack cocaine era, they were separated by tension that took years to heal.

Lyrically, "My Brother's a Basehead," with its plodding drums and looping piano chords, was the clearest Pos had been to that point. Up to then, his lyrics were full of inside jokes and coded language that very few could understand. On "Basehead," he dropped all that to decry drug usage. It was jarring to hear from such a relaxed and presumably happy MC. That was likely the point. You could hear the anger in his voice, the clamoring for past days when weed was the only drug his brother needed. But in 1986, Tyrone "needed a stronger fix" to calm the voices in his head. The song was to be the wake-up call his brother needed.

But think for a second about what Tyrone must've endured: broke and living in a Brooklyn homeless shelter, he couldn't see past his own demons to realize the song's creation was an act of love. "Overall," Tyrone said, "that was the only way my brother had of getting out his frustrations. Anybody on drugs always thinks that they got everything under control, but my actions and my circumstances weren't adding up." The track became one of the most celebrated in the group's discography and was its own act of bravery. In a time when rappers spoke of the drug as a force that couldn't touch them, and with shame for anyone who'd fallen to addiction, Pos was open about how it affected him and that it could happen to anyone. "Looking back on it," he reflected, "he was a good person who had a bad problem."

The group tackled sexual abuse on "Millie Pulled a Pistol on Santa," a song about a young woman who's mistreated by her father. From the outside, it seems her dad is a good man—he dresses up as Santa Claus to entertain kids at the local Macy's—but at night he gets physically violent and rapes her. Yet Millie's friends don't believe her. Left with no choice and wanting the mistreatment to stop, she shoots her father dead in front of the children, leaving them horrified. The song unpacks a persistent plight affecting women: Society tends to blame the survivor when events like these happen, leaving her with no recourse. Then, when she inflicts her own justice, she's vilified by those who never considered her predicament in the first place. Much like "My Brother's a Basehead," "Millie" was courageous and controversial, since these topics weren't discussed openly. *De La Soul Is Dead* was an album of creative risks, a hard reset. It was intense musically and conceptually, and more than thirty years after its release—in an era in which rap is more sanitized and simpler—*De La Soul Is Dead* can be a lot for those who aren't familiar with the era. That's the case with any De La album, really. They aren't passive listens.

De La found themselves in an unusual spot for an act still on the rise. Critics liked these guys. But it's not like the group didn't give the media reasons to question their creative acumen. A jarring title like *De La Soul Is Dead* conjures a permanent demise. Compared with the pastels and rainbows of the first record, the sophomore title was way too morbid. For those unfamiliar with the band's dark sense of humor, the title signaled that maybe these guys were too fussy and not ready for the spotlight. Perhaps the moment was too big and they were better off fading from view. Or maybe they wanted to kill what they constructed and start fresh. Musicians tend to push the envelope around the third or fourth albums, not on the follow-up to a groundbreaking debut. But the decision to shake things up spoke to De La's propensity to go against the grain, even if it cost them fans along the way. *De La Soul Is Dead* was shaping up to be a make-or-break album that could send the band to greater heights or back to the suburbs.

The album wasn't entirely serious; they also poked fun at themselves. On "Bitties in the BK Lounge"—based on a real interaction, according to Charlie Rock—De La jokingly likened themselves to the famed folk singer Tracy Chapman, who, following her hit single "Fast Car," was openly chastised in the Black community for not being Black enough. In the era of hyperaggressive hip-hop and overly sexualized R&B, folk was seen as a white genre that didn't speak at all to the nuances of the Black experience. Historically, as it seemed, folk was, dare I say, "hippy music." Because she was thought to be somewhat soft compared with the brazenness of hip-hop, Chapman was ridiculed for her natural hair and earthy features that accentuated the type of Blackness only seen on the African continent. That level of Blackness wasn't as appreciated then as it is now. In the late '80s, there was a widespread feeling among Black Americans that Africa wasn't a place you could live. US media presented it as impoverished, full of malnourished children with flies in their eyes. And Black Americans invented terms like "African booty scratcher" as a way to denigrate the people from there. Eddie Murphy, in *Eddie Murphy Raw*, had a bit about the fictional character "Mfufu," a poor African woman he said he'd marry because she had no money. The thought was that kinky hair and dark skin constituted struggle, and that thinking permeated other aspects of Black American culture.

This wasn't Chapman performing "Fast Car" at the 2024 Grammys to heartfelt applause. To be associated with Chapman and her class of African-leaning Blackness was a diss in those days, and it seemed De La's self-own wasn't a compliment to her at all. The track also took subtle aim and openly chastised the newfound hangers-on suddenly in De La's orbit. More specifically, it reprimanded the same women who, when the band was broke and unpopular, wouldn't give them the time of day. But when the group says they're not into *them*, the women get indignant: they're bummy and quirky, and can't rap anyway.

De La Soul Is Dead showcased the group's ability to write actual songs with substance without sacrificing the good nature of their debut album. Even the intro was a critical statement: when the announcer Don Newkirk said "Goodnight from *3 Feet High and Rising*," it wasn't just a catchy way into the new album; it was a way out of the old stuff—goodnight, as in good riddance. Critically, *Dead* did better than *3 Feet High* and earned the highest score in the most coveted rap magazine at the time: five mics in *The Source*. In its review, the publication trumpeted the group's ability to relate to wide swaths of listeners at different moments in their lives while remaining centered in the present. Upholding the track "A Roller Skating Jam Named 'Saturdays,'" they said, "It brings out a feeling of letting yourself go on the weekend . . . after a while, you wish you're a part of the fun and madness too." In a positive four-star review for *Rolling Stone*, the critic Scott Poulson-Bryant praised the album's expansiveness, calling it a history of pop experimentalism, with its disparate instruments and samples crashing into each other over the course of its seventy-four-minute runtime. "These three guys have skipped right up to a case of senioritis, coming off like fidgety, ambitious salutatorians rather than the focused valedictorians they could likely become," he wrote. "*De La Soul Is Dead* confirms first that *3 Feet High and Rising* was no fluke and second that these guys are true hip-hop scholars, redefining in jam after jam (with the help of producer Prince Paul) how we listen to, dance to, live with and abide by hip-hop."

Taking aim at well-worn hip-hop tropes—guns, crime, and pimping—*De La Soul Is Dead* was just as groundbreaking as *3 Feet High and Rising* for different reasons: by doubling down on their individuality, they proved once more that rap wasn't just one thing, and that all lyricists had room. That was the real cool: the confidence to disrupt. That lesson applies to all levels of creativity. As long as the work comes from an honest place, it will find the right ears and eyes. The adoration may not arrive right away, but it'll get there when it's supposed to, and last longer. The art will thrive because the integrity is there, and despite it being strange or different, the work lends itself to long-term study. People already have preconceived notions of who you are and what you're supposed to do, and some won't like the work just because. So you might as well create what you're feeling and ignore the doubters. They were never going to support you anyway.

This is yet another lesson I've learned from groups like De La. Over the course of my career, I've become known as the guy who *gets* the odd music that others won't consider. I'll sometimes go up for the albums that other critics have panned, arguing their artistic merits through essays or talks with the actual musicians. That's made me "hard to figure out" and a "disruptor," as one vocalist lovingly called me. I can't and won't fit myself into a box someone else built for me. The audience will catch up eventually. Or maybe they won't. Either way, I can't worry about that.

Looking back at *De La Soul Is Dead*, I'm not sure it was fully understood then or now. I've often wondered if the band was too ahead of their time, or if they got good reviews just because they were liked personally. Even listening to it in today's landscape, where mainstream artists load their albums with tracks as a way to boost streams, *De La Soul Is Dead* can be a slog to get through because of the number of tracks (twenty-seven) and its hour-plus playback. On a practical level, it might be tough for modern listeners to sit still long enough to care about the group's self-deprecating wisecracks and incessant finger-wagging. And *De La Soul Is Dead* sounds like the early '90s—not always in a good way. The beats center stilted hard drum loops and recognizable samples that help passing listeners connect with the music, but such collage-centered work speaks to a time when that production style was preferred. Now, in the 2020s, parts of the album sound dated. Compare that to A Tribe Called Quest: albums like *People's Instinctive Travels and the Paths of Rhythm* and *The Low End Theory* still hold up due to the loose jazz breaks that the group tended to sample. The drums felt airy and dense, almost indebted to an early '70s free jazz band. On *People's Instinctive Travels*, especially, the beats harked back to the earliest days of hip-hop and sounded like what boppers used to breakdance to. As a result, the music endeared itself to hip-hop pioneers and Afrocentric jazz fans who liked sounds with a little more heart and intensity.

De La mastered a different sort of nostalgia. "A Roller Skating Jam Named 'Saturdays'" brought to mind that one school dance or that first kiss with a classmate you'd been crushing on. To younger ears who haven't heard De La and don't have those associations, it wouldn't resonate in an era that may not celebrate the group's sometimes self-indulgent tendency to overstuff their music with bells and whistles. Hip-hop is also an ageist culture that doesn't always celebrate its old heads. Not that De La would ever care about such things. Going against the grain is what they did.

As much as they tried to shrug off fame, you couldn't help but adore De La, even if you didn't fully understand what they were doing. That was part of the allure, the charm, the sleight of hand. Even as they killed themselves creatively, they still spoke to the restless creator in all of us, the ones who ache for respect but still feel jilted by listeners who pine for someone else. They weren't cut-and-dried like their peers; it was the mystery that captivated, the badassery of standing boldly in your identity and letting the ignorant assume they knew what was happening. Without flowers and pastels to attach to, you were forced to sit with Pos, Dave, and Maseo as people, without the veneer of bright Technicolor to mask the real talk. The washed-out black and gray would come to symbolize their art moving forward. Most twenty-year-olds aren't prepared for regular life on their own, let alone one in a fishbowl the likes of which De La had to live in. Though being that self-aware and fully formed was commendable at an age when most young men are thinking about the mall or what party they're headed to, De La had everyone else's happiness to consider. Never mind the fact that they were still growing. The circumstance evokes the public life of other young bands that had to grow publicly.

DE LA SOUL IS A BOY BAND—NOT THE TRADITIONAL KIND OF BOY BAND WE think of and reserve for groups like the Jackson 5, but a boy band nonetheless, taking their parents' old hand-me-downs and flipping them into something new. Almost instantly, De La made tracksuits and Kangol caps feel antiquated—for me, at least. After seeing dudes who weren't *too* much older than me wearing T-shirts and jeans, it made me pine for the same quiet luxury that seemed more affordable. I'm sure my mom appreciated it. I wasn't begging her for the latest Troop jacket or Kool Moe Dee's wraparound Porsche sunglasses. She bought me K-Swiss and British Knights sneakers. Party shirts from JCPenney. It was my job to make it fly (I didn't).

That's the mark of transcendence, where anything that came before you suddenly seems blah, and the vibe you're on becomes the new wave. So it isn't a stretch to liken them to the Jacksons; they upended the status quo the same way. De La wasn't just hip-hop; they were punk, slashing through rhythms and motifs with the energy of Bad Brains, Fishbone, and Death. The music differed, but the attitude was similar.

Across eras and genres, some Black artists spoke to only the coolest among us, ignoring those who didn't have all the designer jewelry, freshest clothes, and expensive shoes. Even jazz had a holier-than-thou air to it. The musicians wore sharp suits and slicked their hair, and the institution around jazz—that is, white people who co-opted the genre into something highbrow and best heard at Carnegie Hall or in a swanky supper club in the Theater District—took the music from the people who created the art in the first place. It got away from economically disadvantaged areas and into the hands of folks who sold it to consumers who could afford pricey tickets and the two-drink minimum. This was part of the crossover appeal with jazz. By the 1960s, it had become so sanitized that it no longer spoke to what was happening outside. It wasn't the counterculture; it was the establishment.

Rap music had a similar complex: a genre that prioritized individuality somehow frowned upon those who didn't look like everyone else. As much as we hail the pioneers for creating room for marginalized people, it somehow looked over the punks and the jazz heads who were just as hip-hop as the prototypical folks in Adidas tracksuits. De La thrived because they made these people feel seen. They saw the cats who were being ignored, the kids who were cool with everyone but didn't run with a particular crew. They addressed the outsiders—the weird yet alluring few. There was an almost unspeakable charm to De La that even the supposedly toughest dudes couldn't ignore, because they respected the crew's idiosyncrasy. There wasn't resentment toward their being raised in the suburbs and coming out ordained by their record label. Rather, their peers looked on with perplexity and admiration. But I've also thought they looked on with a sense of pity, maybe even fear of what their sampling lawsuits meant for the rest of hip-hop. Could De La's issues with sampling open the floodgates for others to police the genre? Was this the excuse nonbelievers needed to deride it? I've always felt that alongside that respect came a sense of relief that De La took those shots first.

Any resentment De La did face came from those beyond the culture who didn't see rap as music and hip-hop as noteworthy. Such claims were rooted in racism and classism, even if the perpetrators didn't want to admit it. They questioned sampling as its own art form because they thought it was easy to mine another person's catalog and repurpose it for their own work. Such thinking ignores the fact that artists have been sampling each other long before De La. What do you think a cover song is? A way to pay homage to the song's originator, yeah? The fact that rap songs weren't re-created with live instruments doesn't make sampling any less viable. Yet as the thinking went, rap producers weren't making actual music. They were pressing buttons and turning knobs. What critics failed to understand was this was high art as well, a new generation of rejectionists like Miles Davis and John Coltrane, who shifted the tide of jazz. Rap marked the first time musicians had discussed crime and socioeconomic politics with such unflinching clarity and didn't tuck it beneath dense poetic layers. I'm not negating artists like Charles Mingus and Nina Simone, who denounced racism and segregation through songs like "Fables of Faubus" and "Mississippi Goddam," but with hip-hop, you didn't have to guess what the artist meant. You didn't have to listen to the way the drums landed or analyze the pain in a saxophone wail. Both the honesty and the art form rankled older musicians who weren't used to hearing such foul language in a creative context. That these kids were repurposing their music—sometimes without pay—was a nonstarter.

Others were cool with it. George Clinton, the founder and lead vocalist of Parliament-Funkadelic, indirectly became the godfather of West Coast hip-hop after the producer Gregory "Big Hutch"

Hutchison dug through his catalog for glossy funk instrumentals to construct his own sound. By sampling Clinton's work, not only did he assemble the foundation of what would be known as G-funk (gangsta funk), but he reintroduced Clinton to a new generation of listeners who only knew him through their parents' record collections. Hutchinson was labelmates with Dr. Dre, who heard the producer's idea and adopted it for his own debut 1992 album, *The Chronic*, which in the decades since its release has become a cornerstone in the foundation of West Coast hip-hop. "If they sampled, they're gonna remember us, and if I get a shot at being remembered, I can make the best use out of it," Clinton once said. In turn, the bandleader forged relationships with the likes of N.W.A, Public Enemy, and OutKast, and even signed a new deal with Brainfeeder Records, the label owned by experimental producer Flying Lotus, in 2016, to make a new album. As of this writing, though, the LP still hadn't come out.

THE TURTLES WEREN'T OK WITH HOW DE LA SAMPLED THEIR SONG "YOU Showed Me" in "Transmitting Live from Mars." "This isn't just a financial objection," said the group's lawyer, Evan Cohen. "[They] are genuinely upset with the way De La Soul chopped up and mutilated their song." People like Mark Volman insist that race wasn't a factor, but there's no denying the vitriol behind such a statement. Would he have that same energy if the suit were against some other rock-influenced act closer to the band's motif? I have no way of knowing that, of course, but history has shown that some rock-and-roll acts, and those in their generation, give passes to those they understand. Music with profanity made by young Black kids was never going to be easily understood. Hell, it still isn't today, sometimes by the people who sign it to their labels. That's not to excuse rappers for taking music that wasn't theirs without permission. If you take Silverman at his word, De La failed to include the Turtles sample in a release form outlining all the songs that were used. If you believe De La, you think it was an oversight on the label's part and that it was on Tommy Boy to make sure all the samples were cleared.

Individual deals were cleared with Clinton, Hall and Oates, and Steely Dan for use of their music, some sweeter than others. Because "Me Myself and I" sampled so heavily from "Knee Deep," Clinton was offered one cent per album, one and two-thirds cents per single, and half the publishing royalties. Conversely, the Turtles were offered a flat fee of one thousand dollars, because, as Tommy Boy put it, the sample was so manipulated it didn't resemble the original track. The rock group likely wouldn't have taken issue if De La had sampled a second or two of their song and not looped substantial sections of it to make a brand-new recording. It was all good when there wasn't much money being made from these songs, but once they began to chart, suddenly sampling was an issue. There's long been this false notion that Black music is disposable and not worthy of protection. But rap producers are no less viable than rock-and-roll musicians, and beatmakers like Hank Shocklee and Prince Paul are just as important as Bob Dylan and Bruce Springsteen. It's "musical collage," as the rapper Daddy-O from Stetsasonic once put it, "the same thing that Andy Warhol did to art."

PART

II

WHEN LIFE IMITATES ART (OR VICE VERSA?)

FOLLOWING THE RELEASE OF *DE LA SOUL IS DEAD*, IT WAS UNCLEAR IF De La would even have a future in the business. Despite the public adoration, the tenor of rap was growing darker, and the pimp-n-crime motif lambasted by the group in '91 wouldn't compare with what was coming. It was a different kind of reality-based rap, one where the sullen nature of Ronald Reagan's America had settled into the next generation of MCs, and the day-to-day of simple existence was an act of revolution. The drugs that the administration trafficked to Black communities, along with the financial stability afforded by it, gave rise to a legion of rappers to talk about selling crack. It was as if all the top MCs wanted to show us how thugged-out they were, how your life didn't compare to theirs, how they could cut you down without a second thought. Suddenly, everyone wanted to be hard, even if their previous work suggested otherwise.

This narrative shift also coincided with a personal shift I was wrestling with. Be it preteen angst or increased awareness of outside stimuli, I didn't feel so upbeat like I had been previously. Around ten was when I started living in my head and thinking about creativity as a career. It coincided with my being labeled "talented and gifted," a school system term given to students who supposedly showed heightened levels of academic proficiency. As a kid, it makes you feel weird. My friends were in the so-called regular classes, and I didn't see myself as different. Still, once a week, I was pulled from my regular routine and relocated to an advanced class—either the only one or one of two Black students in there. It was the first time I felt othered.

I was still young enough to want to be a professional basketball player or doctor when I grew up, but I was also learning to be practical. Maybe I wouldn't grow to be six-foot-nine with a crazy jump shot. Instead, I found myself wondering why certain songs sound the way they do and why sad ones tend to feel better on rainy days. Mood music sat with me longer than the latest up-tempo dance track, and rap—especially the morose style that mostly came from the West Coast in the early '90s—spoke loudest to me. While the approach brought us lots of great work, there was no denying how bleak the '90s were musically. From groups like Mobb Deep and Onyx to megastars like Wu-Tang Clan and the LA-based Death Row Records, grit and grime were the most important aspects of hip-hop, even if it had dire consequences midway through the decade.

The despair felt more ingrained, not outward-looking like the rap of the previous decade. Rappers were taking stock of what was happening around them, internalizing it, and presenting it as news—no different than what broadcasters do on the front lines of war-torn countries. But where those acts were seemingly asking for a lifeline in the wake of racist government practices, the next generation flipped that hopelessness into something less anguished, fostering an era of MCs that appealed to Italian mobster films like *Goodfellas* and *The Godfather* and cocaine-centered narratives like *Scarface*. Take Nas, for instance: his debut album *Illmatic* detailed the austerity of 1990s Queens. Its anguish became the basis of something positive: the monster created by society gave Nas the tough exterior needed to navigate New York City.

The same went for the Notorious B.I.G., the MC from Brooklyn whose flamboyance made him a pop star and whose propensity for violent rhymes foretold his shooting death in 1997. That's not to say that his demise was karma—*quite* the opposite—but his narrative, along with the beef he had with the Los Angeles–based firebrand Tupac Shakur, became the cornerstone of hip-hop's story in the '90s, that the genre had strayed from its roots, and maybe the gangster/mafioso motif had gone too far. It's one thing to glamorize thug shit in your music; it's another to see the consequences of it play out in real life.

Where did a group like De La Soul fit into all of this? The short answer is they didn't, but the looming overcast of hip-hop in the early '90s found them too, even if they didn't associate with what their peers were doing. Their attitudes downshifted as well. While *De La Soul Is Dead* was largely a response to the marketing of *3 Feet High and Rising*, the trio just seemed a lot darker, almost gangsta rap–adjacent. Between the fights that were becoming legend and the jaded nature of the music itself, the brothers were teetering. "It was a load of bullshit on which I prefer not to look back," Maseo once said. "Especially the stuff with the Turtles. Luckily everything is cleared now, but these things wear you down."

It can also stall your momentum if you let it, and De La wasn't the type of act that you understood right away. They still needed time to

61

simmer and improve, and it was tough to even think about that with everything else happening. It's also lonely to be seen and beloved but also misunderstood and misinterpreted. No one prepares you for the mix of bewilderment and intrigue that comes with being a unicorn, the feeling that no matter how accepted you seem to be, you're still on an island—a one of one. And that's where De La stood in the early '90s: a band to themselves who people revered but didn't get, a squad trying to navigate the road less traveled as listeners drifted toward gangsta rap. It's not easy to redefine what rap music can sound like. It's harder when your ripple crashes into a tidal wave just as you're getting started.

But here's the thing about setting trends: not everyone appreciates it while it's happening. Sure, you can be acknowledged in passing, but it isn't until the public has had time to ruminate that you're given the credit you deserve. But De La had been fighting this reality since the beginning, and even more once *De La Soul Is Dead* made its way through popular music. Did gangsta rap enthusiasts feel weird about playing their music publicly? Did they play their music at all? Did they treat it as taboo, as something they only played on low volumes on headphones in the apartment under a blanket? Or did they trumpet them loudly? Was their weirdness embraced by those types? The answer to all these questions was probably yes. The easy retort was that everyone loved De La, or at least respected what they were trying to do. It was complicated.

"If you asked me whether the new CD has been received as well as the first one, I could answer yes and no," Maseo admitted then. "My mates, the younger listeners, like it. The older ones, the people who really loved the sound of 'Me Myself and I' and 'Say No Go,' are a little disappointed, I think, but I don't care because they please me. Most people don't have the vibe they had for De La Soul in the early days, but there are also people who initially were holding back a bit and who are getting into us now."

De La's momentum slowed following their second album, but it had nothing to do with their music; it was due to a shift in the audience's palate. Perception was everything, so it maybe wasn't the best look in a hypermasculine climate to blast "Ring Ring Ring (Ha Ha Hey)" and "A Roller Skating Jam Named 'Saturdays'" from the car. Even in their toughest times, their work tried to find some semblance of light within a world and industry that don't always give shine to it. Even as they were being "worn down," per Maseo's statement, their financial and creative struggles were such that one would've understood if they walked away altogether.

MC SERCH TRAVELED WITH THEM IN THE LATE 1980S. HE'D TALK ABOUT HOW practical they were—that, while others may have celebrated the spoils of fame by splurging on hotel suites and expensive meals, they operated as middle-class workers who didn't see the need for such things. Even then, De La opted for the long view, plugging along slowly in hopes of sticking around longer. As sudden popularity dictated a rapid rise for the trio, they pushed against the flameout that befell others in the same position. "We were talking about driving Maseratis and being with bad chicks in reggae clubs, and that was our shit," the 3rd Bass lyricist told me. "They were really on some 'Me Myself and I,' self-identification, self-love, self-preservation of a culture. And we were preserving the culture, but at the same time just really enjoying the elements of the culture that were cool, sexy, and powerful."

Back then, he said, rappers were free to be unique creators without the knee-jerk judgment of social media and hot-take criticism. As a result, others tried to emulate De La and fell woefully short of the band's one-of-a-kind presence. Aside from Tribe, the only other group that came close in the '90s was the Pharcyde, the LA-based unit that rose to prominence thanks to "Passin' Me By," a lovelorn song with a memorable hook and a jazz-centered backbeat that became a commercial hit. On the band's sophomore album, 1995's *Labcabincalifornia*, they linked with an unknown beatmaker named James "Jay Dee" Yancey, whose combination of esoteric samples from here, there, and everywhere and patchwork drum programming gave the music a lived-in essence, like a band onstage improvising in real time (more on that later).

Linking with De La for a tour through Europe, 3rd Bass—themselves a popular group signed to Def Jam Records—stayed in expensive hotels and drove luxury cars. "We're staying at the InterContinental Hotel outside Piccadilly Circus," Serch said. "I can't even imagine what those rooms were worth." One night, they visited De La, thinking, well, it's De La, for sure they're staying at this pricey spot on a different floor. Nope; they took up residence at some run-of-the-mill spot. "They showed us a room with a bathroom and three beds, twin beds, and they were making way more money than we were and this is where they were staying," Serch said. "And I got on some fly shit and I said, 'Yo, y'all the headliners. What the fuck y'all staying in here for?'" Pos turned to Serch: "'Yeah, but I'm going to have InterContinental money twenty years after this tour is over.' And I said, 'Yeah and so am I.' He said, 'Maybe, but I'll know I have my money.' Those guys were just smart businessmen."

That common sense also typified the way they handled their careers going forward. Instead of chasing the summit of their first LP, they focused on creative intent, building a catalog of albums that were vastly different from each other yet similar in scope. They all served to present the full picture of De La Soul, the sometimes surly, occasionally reflective crew with real life at the forefront. In a genre full of veneer and larger-than-life characters, De La Soul felt attainable, real dudes with emotional scars.

Could they out-rap you? Sure, but if they weren't lyricists, they looked like people you'd see working in a Sam Goody, or just others in a sea of nameless faces you walk past every day. They were working-class survivors who rapped about the nuances of everyday life in ways that felt familiar and messy and smart. Like us, they were trying to figure it out as it came, rolling with the punches while making us think and laugh along the way. They were flawed and fly as fuck for no reason. They reminded me of neighborhood locals who could smoke weed and talk shit with the tough guys, but when the tough guys went to do tough-guy things, they were dissuaded from tagging along. People like Pos, Dave, and Maseo have friends who protect and appreciate their uniqueness and see the potential they have to reach greater plateaus. They respect the clothes, the dialect, the hip-hop meets jazz-bohemian aesthetic, the "We're nice guys but don't fuck with us" demeanor. Then and always, De La was going to be De La.

I know this because I came up the same way. I used to hang with friends who weren't always down to do the right things but were good people at heart. I'd drink underage, smoke weed, and go to the mall with these guys, but on a Friday night when it was time to go *out* out, I'd be home recording songs from the radio, talking on the phone, and playing cassettes and CDs. I don't know who to credit more: my friends for seeing something in me that I didn't see in myself or my mother for keeping me away from nonsense. My mom had this knack for saying no to all the right requests, though in the moment I didn't know why I couldn't go to that party or walk across the highway to the still-developing neighborhood. My friends were going there and I wanted to go too. Yet somehow she was still liberal enough to let me figure out life with limited barriers. But my friends knew how to say no as well, their denials coming with a different flair: *Man, I dunno if this is your thing; you should go home and write.* Throughout history, there were various people like me and De La who wanted to explore and get into trouble, yet there was always someone there to keep us on track. It's love in its purest form, to want the best for someone else unconditionally and to protect those people even at the risk of your own peace. That's what my folks did for me, and I can tell that's what happened with Pos, Dave, and Maseo. Real recognize real and all that. Certain people just emit light. They're gonna do something with their art and shift culture somehow. Even as worldly struggles came down on De La, they maintained their glow. Their truest fans held them down when others wouldn't.

Still, amid declining sales and diminished cultural currency, they were able to hang around due to the diversity of their catalog—by meeting listeners where they were in their lives. As we got older, De La got older, and they weren't trying to present themselves as anything other than who they were. Where others might try to act like they're still the younger versions of themselves, De La wasn't afraid to grow up. They embraced adulthood, exercising the youthful spirit of inexperienced artists who didn't know better. The best artists also know how to push their listeners to the brink without pushing them over the edge. With each album, there's some new creative wrinkle, some subtle shift in the production or narrative arc that inspires cultural discourse months and years down the road. De La did that naturally, by simply living life and putting those experiences in the music.

De La made me feel seen as someone who was cool with the rough-and-tumble sect but also the music nerds, the English lit squad, and the slam poetry crew. They wrote the blueprint on how to be well-rounded human beings in the public space, and how not to be an asshole to strangers who support you, a skill I'd need deep into my career. They were the nice guys who finished first; with them, the notion that compassionate people are used and underappreciated became a misconception—mostly.

But how do you keep your soul in an industry that aims to chip away at it? How do you maintain peace and sensibility on such a public perch? What keeps a smile on your face when some around you want to test your resolve, simply because you're different or nice? The answer, in most cases, is to bend to the wills and expectations of strangers as a way to fit societal norms. But De La was too inscrutable and highbrow at times, their music a bit too heady, their aesthetic confusing.

At a 1992 show at the Ritz in Manhattan, in particular, a *New York Times* critic dinged the band for taking the fun out of their performance and resorting to tough-guy posturing that made them like everyone else. "What once made De La Soul special was that it offered a lighthearted alternative," wrote Karen Schoemer in her concert review. There were those who wondered if De La had already lost their way, whether *3 Feet High and Rising* was a fluke and the critical acclaim for *De La Soul Is Dead* wasn't deserved. If, as Schoemer pointed out, listeners were losing interest, it would be tough to split the difference between two vastly different records like those—one with such bliss, the other washed out and bleak. We celebrate De La Soul now, but the albums *3 Feet High* and *De La Soul Is Dead* didn't offer clear views into who they were as people. They weren't the hippy thing, but who were they, really? A mash-up of conflicting looks and sounds, a confluence of ideas and ingredients that could've easily spoiled the meal. But because they zagged when others zigged, they naturally drew attention, and by the early '90s, even De La was swept up in the pack, they offered just enough to keep ahead of it.

When you're a child, as I was in the mid-1980s, you don't want to be associated with anything the elders in your family might dig. You think everything is new—because, well, everything is—and you don't have the sense of history that others have. Whatever you hear is the first and coolest, and there's no realizing that the rap you're listening to now comes from older source material. So it was cool that De La Soul was paying homage to a once-forgotten genre like jazz, at one point the epitome of cool in the Black community.

Whatever the genre, old heads have problems with music they

can't understand. The new thing is somehow detrimental, and we replicate the chatter of curmudgeons past, painting it with the same broad brush the OGs did. Because jazz had become smooth and didn't differentiate from quiet storm R&B, it wasn't seen as the voice of Black people. So noted musicians like Ron Carter and Art Blakey sat on the shelf until the Native Tongues pulled them down, dusted them off, and repurposed them. Before jazz enjoyed a resurgence in the '80s, it was a dead art form that rap listeners didn't care about. De La helped make jazz intriguing for listeners who only knew about it as a cursory sound.

By the time the group rose to prominence, rap was the end-all be-all for young Black kids who had things to say but weren't given the agency to speak up. The brilliance of *De La Soul Is Dead* lies in the concurrency of lyrics and sounds. Though the music was polychromatic, the rhymes were more straightforward, which led to deeper, and more accurate, critical dissection. It dropped the vernacular of previous work for a plainspoken narrative. But instead of hearing a well-worn sample, you heard these weird drum breaks and muted horns, as if they didn't even bother to clean the vinyl before repurposing it. Such subtlety gave the album a distinct character, making the music feel tactile and lived in, like a worn record with all the cracks and pops on it. They made it OK to live with mistakes on record, to spin the imperfections of the source material into a positive. Through their use of jazz, De La showed that it was fine to loosen up—not just lyrically but sonically.

It's like the Roots' bandleader Ahmir "Questlove" Thompson once said: De La—and A Tribe Called Quest after them—opened the door to "digging culture" in hip-hop. De La didn't sample anything obvious. Because of them, we ran, biked, caught the bus, whatever, to the local record store and went straight for the jazz section, in hopes of catching just a glimpse of what De La was hearing. But a funny thing happens when you start collecting jazz albums: you can't stop.

One cornerstone album leads to another, then another. Then you start reading the liner notes and notice this and that person played on it, leading you to seek out their discographies. Then that leads to more discovery, and more albums. De La Soul birthed generations of crate-diggers who, like them, wanted to soak in cool music from everywhere. Like their listeners, De La believed good music was good music, no matter what genre the industry deemed it, no matter when it was released. Without *De La Soul Is Dead*, Questlove declared, the then-sixteen-year-old Dilla likely would've skipped past the Ahmad Jamal song he used to create the title track of De La's 1996 album *Stakes Is High*. And I can't imagine that track without those blaring horns, announcing the group's triumphant return—that time from a three-year hiatus.

Dilla might be the most famous example, but he wasn't the only direct disciple of De La's sonic experimentation. Questlove himself has leaned into the imperfections of jazz and soul as a producer and drummer, sometimes dragging the kick just a little, giving the music an imbalance. That woozy aesthetic goes back to Dilla, which goes back to De La. While the beats feel slightly off-kilter or, for music aficionados, just flat-out wrong, there's no denying the spirit of it. Obscure jazz pairing with the otherness of distilled drums and vocal sampling made De La feel foreign, familiar yet distant.

There's a producer like Otis "Madlib" Jackson Jr., who in the mid-2000s amassed a cult following due to his exceptional ability as a crate-digging curator and jazz student. His father was a jazz vocalist, so he was born into the genre's tradition, but his propensity for arcane samples and heavy use of jazz was greatly influenced by De La Soul. "I grew up on them dudes," he once said. "That album actually changed my production. That's kind of where my whole style for Quasimoto [his rapping alter ego] came from." Moreover, Madlib's oddball aesthetic—the weird audio collage and pitched-up rapping—was another page ripped from their book. Like them,

Madlib pulls from everything—comedy albums, blaxploitation films, random dialogue from various audio sources—and pieces it all into a patchwork tapestry of psychedelic beats and occasional rapping, sometimes about the pleasures of weed, other times about nothing at all. Madlib's love of jazz even led him to create the fictional band Yesterdays New Quintet, invent made-up alter egos, and craft music based on the alter ego at the helm.

De La also influenced a generation of underground beatmakers and rappers, artists like Quelle Chris, Open Mike Eagle, and R.A.P. Ferreira, to craft equally off-center hip-hop meant to defy what the genre was supposed to be. Like De La, these artists bristled at how others defined their music, because it wasn't just one thing. It was hip-hop and jazz with elements of R&B and a psychedelic aura. Its inability to be classified made it tough to fully assess what was happening, but the capacious aspects of the work ensured its long-term viability in experimental spaces. But that wasn't the only way De La influenced hip-hop. They made skits popular.

DURING THE MAKING OF *3 FEET HIGH AND RISING*, PRINCE PAUL SUGGESTED the idea of creating the *3 Feet High and Rising Game Show*, a short that would serve as the album's narrative backbone. Pos, Dave, and Maseo had already tinkered with what they called "bug-out pieces" as an excuse to act silly in their home studio. In turn, Paul's idea to re-create a game show for the band's debut album was met with excitement—or, better yet, ease. "Rap records always had some dialogue in them, like, 'Hey man, I'm gonna' smack you in the face,' or 'Yo . . . let's get it!' but they weren't sketches with a whole vibe to them," Paul once said. "We did it to fill that void, to give our album some structure. It was just something we tried out and it evolved. We never thought it would become a rap album staple."

For *De La Soul Is Dead*, the band created a story about teenage bullies harassing younger children in a schoolyard over a De La Soul cassette they found in the trash. In the opening skit especially, the band let listeners know right away how they felt about the current state of hip-hop. None of this was scripted ahead of time; just like they'd done for *3 Feet High and Rising*, the band hit record and let the silliness take over. "After we finished recording, we just picked a day to do the skits. We had the concept of kids in the schoolyard and got Mista Lawnge from Black Sheep, a few friends, and their nieces and nephews," Paul continued. "It was always the same: nothing written, all off the top of the head. Sketch improv-style like comics performing in the subway."

Comedy was another underrated aspect of De La's influence. Before the likes of the game show and the schoolyard scene, and even a complete miss like "De La Orgee," hip-hop was almost entirely stone-faced. With De La's arrival, irreverence followed; their blend of comedy was more *Animal House* than George Carlin sociopolitical commentary. The skits weren't there to make you think deeply or reconsider your position on the world. It was reality-based rap set in an alternate reality. They wanted to make us laugh or, at the very least, forget about whatever ailed us beyond the music. If their art was meant to be an escape, then the skits were rest stops along the road to some sort of peace, depending on what that meant for the listener.

In that way, De La Soul could be refreshing and juvenile and enlightening all at once, equally cringe and "aha!" That made every De La project an experiment and a test: their approach to skits was to throw everything against the wall and see what sticks, no different than a comedian at the Comedy Cellar working out material in a late-night set. But where a comic like Eddie Murphy or Chris Rock might take the strongest jokes and scrap the rest, De La leaned into all of it, all of the silliness, all of the irreverence, all of the knuckleheaded, sophomoric hijinks that mature adults considered too juvenile for artists their ages. De La's use of skits made their albums feel panoramic. Listeners could choose their own adventure. If you wanted, on *De La Soul Is Dead* you could just as easily follow the story of the discarded De La tape and laugh at the name-calling and pop culture references.

I can hear the same reckless abandon in an artist like Redman, the New Jersey lyricist whose comedic rhymes about smoking weed and fornication made him a fan favorite. But where De La's aura rang psychedelic, Redman's felt cruder, a bit boorish. In his most prosperous period, from 1992 to 2001, he took on the character of Sooperman Luva, a dude from around the way who flies and has X-ray vision like Superman, but he smokes blunts, has sex with all the women, and lives the life of a pimp. Though the character wouldn't rate in today's climate of social reckoning, Sooperman was a beloved figure across albums like *Dare Iz a Darkside* and *Muddy Waters*; we needed to hear how the story continued and just how absurd the situation would become. The same went for the rap group Little Brother, whose 2005 album *The Minstrel Show* incorporated a large number of skits for its narrative. The album followed the imagined programming of a Black television network, and the skits operated as commercial breaks between songs. Not since De La had skits been blended so seamlessly into an album, to the point where *The Minstrel Show* doesn't hold up without them. That all stems from the creative risk that De La took years prior.

The band's creative influence went beyond music, though. I also hear the band's irreverence surface in the comedic output of Dave Chappelle. In the mid-'90s, he started making waves in his native Washington, DC, and beyond as a fresh observer who unpacked the craziness of everyday life with a childlike wonder that landed somewhere between the mundane and the extraordinary. With Chappelle, a bit about a cab ride through the ghetto leads to a punch line about a baby selling crack to support his kids. A film like *Half Baked*, where a man gets arrested for feeding junk food to a horse and his friends sell pilfered medical weed to bail him out, draws comparisons to De La's own sophomoric bits. Such boundary pushing lent itself to the creation of *Chappelle's Show* in 2003, a cultural landmark series that gave us characters like Clayton Bigsby (a blind Black white supremacist), Tyrone Biggums (a neighborhood crackhead), and Ashy Larry (a gambling addict who'd shoot dice in his underwear without wearing any lotion). Critics bristled at the audacity of Chappelle's comedy, a foretelling of the fire-starting run of stand-up specials he'd perform twenty years later. But as much as we grimaced at the no-holds-barred nature of Chappelle's work on the Comedy Central show, we couldn't look away. We laughed at the political incorrectness, snickering quietly (or loudly) at the immaturity. But that's also why we loved it, and why we loved De La Soul. They tapped into an innocence many of us had locked away and forgotten about. Not only did they make it OK to be abundantly creative, but they forced us to have fun, to laugh like nobody was watching, to crack jokes in public spaces in mixed company, to love on each other without the worry of judgment from strangers. Their jokes induced head-back, mouth-wide-open LOLs, the type of laughter only shared with the closest loved ones.

The band's peak unfolded between the late '80s and the mid-'90s, with the advent of compact discs, which allowed eighty minutes of music to be stored on them, and musicians of all types took advantage of the burgeoning format, sometimes oversaturating their albums with filler simply because they could. Years later, in the 2010s, at the height of the streaming era, musicians took advantage of the infinite space offered by the Internet by releasing long "albums" (which mostly felt like collections of songs with no coherent theme or focus) to boost play counts. Certainly, there was some of this going on back in De La's era. Listening to *3 Feet High and Rising* and *De La Soul Is Dead* with older, less patient ears can be a struggle. Yet the humor translates;

it's both a time capsule and a reset. For instance, in 2000, on the band's fifth studio album, *Art Official Intelligence: Mosaic Thump*, De La opted for the more serious-minded "ghost weed" skits. Though still comedic, the concept went like this: by smoking this particular strain of marijuana, novice rappers could take on the voice and flow of professional lyricists, impressing their friends in the process. One of the rappers featured on the skit was Pharoahe Monch, the Queens-raised lyricist whose technical prowess and intricate wordplay made him one of the most celebrated rappers in the industry. When Pos called Pharoahe and broke down the skit idea, his involvement was a no-brainer. "I was like, 'Unbelievable,'" Pharoahe told me laughing over the phone. "He was like, 'Write something that's you, that's distinctively Pharoahe Monch, and come to the studio.' I still didn't know how they were gonna flip it until I heard the final product. It's infamous, man. People are still on social media like, 'Ghost weed! Ghost weed!'"

That De La's comedy can elicit this type of reaction twenty years on is a flex, even as their music was kept off streaming platforms. As fans traded their music with each other and others quietly ripped full albums from YouTube, the comedy persisted. The music might fade, its relevance twisting and shifting as rap evolves, but the feel-good aspects of De La's humor remain intact. Laughter, like music, is a universal language.

While De La popularized the use of skits in rap music, their approach harked back to old comedy albums of the '60s and '70s, when listeners could hear stalwarts like Redd Foxx and Richard Pryor on vinyl in their living rooms. Revolution breeds revolution, and it's safe to say that Prince Paul and the members of De La were inspired by the raunchy rapport of Foxx and Pryor, or even the slapstick originality of Steve Martin. But on Laff Records, which distributed the Foxx and Pryor albums, along with equally bawdy ones by LaWanda Page and "Auntie" Tina Dixon, listeners got to hear the live sets that weren't sanctioned for mass consumption. Their albums were taboo to listen to—especially for underage children laughing quietly when their parents weren't around—but it's from these records that legends would emerge, as well as comic-minded musicians like De La Soul. Comedy is meant to be rebellious, to rankle the status quo. When done correctly, there's a before and an after, as was the case with Richard Pryor, widely considered the greatest comedian of all time. De La Soul is of that same ilk; they represent that pivotal moment when hip-hop and comedy started to merge in the late '80s. They, like Pryor and Foxx before them, stand at the intersection of then and now, and they have endured in a cold genre that doesn't honor its heroes—until it's too late. But listening to De La was almost like listening to a comedy album, but with dope and innovative music as the soundtrack. The band and their counterparts used skits to mock gangsta rap, a risky move, certainly, but one that was necessary to maintain balance.

Much like the music alongside it, there was a certain "What the fuck" quality to the skits, an indescribable joy that emanated from the art. But that's what distinguishes it. Because De La embarked upon a sound and aesthetic we hadn't heard before. Therefore we couldn't fully explain why they hit us so hard, why they made us laugh so deeply. The skits gave us something we didn't know we needed at the time: absurdity, fortitude. For kids like me and my older cousin Isaac—who, at six years my senior, was the first Black person I'd ever seen ride a skateboard in a middle-class enclave like Landover—De La Soul made popular what we were into.

Through De La, I didn't have to code-switch; they got me and I got them. Thirty years later, as the physical laughs have digitized, the comedy they exuded still strikes a chord. While the hysteria has worn off and the band has become a legacy act surviving on the goodwill of fans and big-name supporters, the comedic integrity remains. As society bleakens and the US remains deeply divided along political and ideological lines, De La's still conjures a smile, the memory of days gone by when my life was a lot simpler. It also helped me feel normal at a time when others started treating me differently. Surely I was thankful for such love from friends and family, but to hear De La laugh in the face of such seriousness put life in perspective. It also solidified their humanity: emerging from uncertainty when the path looks dubious is something we all have to do.

GETTIN' GROWN

F YOU HANG AROUND LONG ENOUGH, YOU'LL COME TO A FORK IN THE ROAD.
Your third or fourth album will be the vaunted "make-or-break"
record, because impatient executives want to see more from you.
In most cases, the artist or band is moving along just fine. Their fans
still love them, tickets are selling, and the albums keep flying out the
door. But there's a notion that maybe the artist is losing steam, or,
more accurately, the execs are getting bored as the newness wears off.
The artist is no longer the trophy that the bigwigs can parade around
the office. De La Soul found themselves in this position in 1993,
when the rap culture they knew, and helped create, was basically dead.
Folks weren't trying to be happy anymore; it was time to talk about

some real shit. Or at least some weird and demonic shit. Horrorcore rap became a thing, thanks to rappers like Kool Keith, who openly killed his peers (metaphorically, of course) as early as 1988, on the Ultramagnetic MCs' debut album, *Critical Beatdown*.

Three years later, the Santa Ana, California, group KMC (Kaotic Minds Curruptin) also performed horrorcore on their LP *Three Men with the Power of Ten*, on aptly named songs like "Terrifying Tracks," "Murder," and "Grim Reaper." A darker, more biting version of the gangsta rap that sprouted from the West Coast in the late '80s, horrorcore was a manifestation of the torment emanating from the sometimes fatal interactions with the Los Angeles Police Department, along with the simmering bitterness due to poorly distributed resources to the city's Black and brown communities.

Though the group was short-lived and didn't release another album, their willingness to go there influenced other West Coast rappers. Yet the true champions of this subgenre resided in the American South—in Houston, Texas, and Memphis, Tennessee. Horrorcore was made popular by the Geto Boys and Three 6 Mafia. The former delved into the mental health challenges of living while Black in America; the latter employed ominous sonic cues and satanic imagery to convey unrelenting gloom. Gravediggaz, a supergroup of sorts featuring Wu-Tang Clan leader the RZA and Prince Paul, brought this sound back east in 1994; their album *6 Feet Deep* would become a cult classic.

Ironically, Gravediggaz formed out of contempt for Tommy Boy Records: the RZA was once signed there under the name Prince Rakeem and was frustrated with the lack of push his music had gotten. The same went for Paul. The two met in 1988 when Paul was producing *3 Feet High and Rising*. "We made demos together and I thought he was an amazing lyricist, but I lost contact with him," Paul once said. "When I started coming up with the idea for the Gravediggaz at the end of 1990, he was one of the first people I thought of."

Indirectly, De La was tied to the gloom that would consume hip-hop culture in the mid-'90s, and this melancholy permeated the music they were making around that time. Gravediggaz harbored the same heady aesthetic as De La, but it allowed Paul to exorcise creative demons that had been bubbling under the surface. Bearing icepicks and shovels and sporting black and gray finery suited for undertakers, Gravediggaz wanted to resurrect the mentally dead—the same sort of over-the-top rap nerdery that De La embodied, albeit on a brighter side of the spectrum.

Who could blame Paul, though? A talent like his shouldn't have to audition, especially given his credentials. The bad blood flowed throughout the creaking, clattering beats he cocreated with RZA. On songs like "Nowhere to Run, Nowhere to Hide," direct shots were taken at midlevel record execs who didn't see their vision. "And to the A&R who couldn't understand the product," went a line from the track, "now look who's on top." So Paul wasn't in the right creative frame to assist with De La moving forward. His anger was beginning to come out too much in the music. De La was more apt to suppress their grievances, which made it all the more shocking when they spoke of them directly. They would address those issues on their third album, *Buhloone Mindstate*, which they started recording in 1992 amid interpersonal group turmoil within the Native Tongues collective. For a group with such promise and love from the masses, their end was just as swift as their beginning, and they would come to a crashing halt right before our eyes.

From the outside looking in, it seemed like everything was all good between the members: De La was still chugging along, and A Tribe Called Quest had reached noteworthy status thanks to two critically acclaimed albums—1990's *People's Instinctive Travels and the Paths of Rhythm*, and 1991's *The Low End Theory*—along with the forthcoming 1993 album *Midnight Marauders*, which to many listeners put Tribe in the Greatest of All Time category, eclipsing De

La Soul. People reacted differently to Tribe; they seemed more fun and open-ended, kinda like De La during the *3 Feet High and Rising* days. Tribe projected optimism and light, freedom and structure commingling among jazz and funk. Unlike De La, Tribe doled out their sound in bite-sized chunks, carefully peeling it back, making it easier to listen to. Part of the reason why some listeners didn't fully embrace *De La Soul Is Dead* is because, well, it was a lot. And sometimes the vitriol got old.

By sampling the sweetest parts of artists like Minnie Riperton and Art Blakey, Tribe tapped into a saccharine nostalgia, conjuring memories of that first kiss or that first slow dance with that girl you liked. After a while, Tribe made people feel better than De La did. Those in the know understand why—shitty record deals and bad marketing and all—but, quite frankly, there's only so many times you can relisten to De La calling someone "cocksnot" and telling us they can fight.

On the song "I Am I Be," from *Buhloone Mindstate*, Pos lamented the broken state of the Native Tongues, holding himself and his collaborators accountable for letting the collective falter due to egos. "Or some tongues who lied and said, 'We'll be natives to the end,' nowadays we don't even speak," he rapped. "I guess we got our own life to live / Or is it because we want our own kingdom to rule?" Each of the Native Tongues members were stars in their own right. De La and Tribe aside, Jungle Brothers also enjoyed a certain stature: without them, there is no De La or Tribe, no path for Afrocentric rap or so-called alternative hip-hop. Elsewhere, the rap duo Black Sheep gathered steam thanks to the hit song "The Choice Is Yours," which was heard damn near everywhere upon its release.

The same went for the British rapper Monie Love, whose 1990 song "Monie in the Middle" became a fun-loving phenomenon that populated dance floors long after its release during the Native Tongues' infancy. Then there was Queen Latifah, a celebrated MC who championed women in ways others hadn't in rap music. Sporting kufi hats, West African clothing, and medallions, and with songs like "Ladies First" and "Evil That Men Do," Latifah was fearless and forceful, a no-bullshit, respect-commanding lyricist. She would be the biggest star of any of them, a multihyphenate polymath whose stardom shone on television and in films, and picked up gold statues along the way. As it were, this iteration of the Native Tongues wasn't supposed to last long; perhaps the star power was too bright. In a group of alphas, all of whom were making intriguing music that started conversations and shifted culture, there wasn't enough room at the top for everyone.

In collectives like these, there has to be at least one leader. In the Staten Island–bred Wu-Tang Clan, for instance, all roads lead to the RZA, the group's founder and architect. Even in the Soulquarians— which, with its peace-and-love ethos, was made in the Native Tongues image—Questlove was thought to be the group's leader, much to the chagrin of at least one of its members.

The demise of the Native Tongues was devastating. On one hand, friends fall out all the time; it's just a way of life. But the Native Tongues felt like my tribe, and who else was gonna fill the void? Where else could I go to hear about space and women's empowerment and Black pride from one crew? When you're young, you think your favorites belong to you, and how dare they mature and grow apart or just be plain-ol' human beings with self-doubts and insecurities? They can't evolve beyond what we want them to be—if they do, they've somehow betrayed us. That's how it felt when Pos revealed publicly that all wasn't right with them.

The source of the tension came from Pos, Q-Tip, and Afrika Baby Bam and a supposed misunderstanding between the three, something about this person not treating that person correctly, and this person thinking they're family when others did not. It all seemed hazy and not a good reason to be at odds. "[It's] about how I felt, we were friends, but in terms of being friends you're supposed to treat each other like family and brothers as opposed to what I thought maybe they weren't," Pos once said. As you can see, the reasons were convoluted.

That Pos didn't want to fully discuss why the collective splintered also addressed why De La has been able to persist all these years. The lack of a clear answer spoke to a loyalty that he had to the band and other members of the Native Tongues. De La's disagreements have always been kept in-house; years later, Pos would say he regretted saying the little he did say on "I Am I Be." He still had love and respect for Tip and Baby Bam as people and musicians.

The rest of *Buhloone Mindstate* wrestled with the notion of blowing up but not going pop. In the era of MC Hammer, artists made waves from synthesized rap that took broader listenership into account, and songs like "U Can't Touch This" didn't feel like the genuine article. De La had already dealt with something similar in '89 with the success of "Me Myself and I" and had vowed to never return to that. On that song, one could hear definitive talent but it didn't encapsulate the full breadth of what De La was. By the time *Buhloone Mindstate* came around, they were shooting down hip-hop tropes by name, openly scoffing at monetary excess and thug posturing while stopping just short of naming the perpetrators.

The video for "Ego Trippin' (Part Two)" was the most egregious example: From the outset, we see three shirtless dudes wearing jewelry and drifting images of a black Mercedes-Benz convertible. Maseo's wearing a headdress made of American cash, and Dave pulls up to a fancy house that isn't really his. The video broke the fourth wall and spoke directly to viewers about the mythologies of hip-hop culture. You mean rappers aren't as rich as they claim? They're not pulling all the hottest women in the club? Those gold chains are rented? Then there was the bald, topless guy in the video wearing dark sunglasses and ornate jewelry. It could've been anyone. Tupac thought it was about him and got pissed. Not long before, Pac had released a video for his song "I Get Around," where he paraded around a palatial estate—shirtless and flanked by women—in a party-like atmosphere. Pac thought De La was mocking him, and, as Pac was prone to do, he later addressed De La head-on, rapping, "De La got a problem with this hard shit / Ever since 'Me Myself and I' y'all been garbage."

Tides were turning for De La; this was the first time someone fired back. They sometimes toed the line between acceptable and arrogant, and anything they didn't consider "real hip-hop" was skewered and looked down upon. As they got older, they got grumpier, and the barbs didn't land the same with their peers or listeners. The audience was changing. They were changing too, but not always for the better. At a point, you have to think back to your younger days and remember that you're the same person who used to run down the type of music you now like. Around '93 and beyond, De La failed to recall that their way wasn't the golden trail either. That five years prior, they had detractors too. I'm quite sure there were older heads who disliked De La because it wasn't Grandmaster Flash or Doug E. Fresh, so who were they to say what was real and fake or good and bad? What made them the authority on all things dope? Nonetheless, that didn't stop Maseo on "Eye Patch," *Buhloone Mindstate*'s intro. "I'd like to give a shout-out to all those rappers who dissed us on record," he deadpanned, "and I wanna let you know you're still wack."

Tupac wasn't wrong, though. There was a feeling that by '93 De La had leveled off. Hell no they weren't garbage, and they didn't have serious issues with gangsta rap, but they did take issue with what felt inauthentic. If you were really about shooting up the block and dealing drugs? Cool. Who were they to judge? But if you grew up in a properly developed neighborhood, went to college, and suddenly took on a Colombian or Italian nickname because you watched mob films, then they had smoke. Still, what they failed to understand as they progressed was that they couldn't keep poking the bear and not expect pushback. The barbs are fine when you're seemingly untouchable; not so much when you fall closer to Earth. They don't land with the same ferocity. Maybe it's just human nature, but people get sick of the finger-pointing and condemnation: artists want to do what they do, and listeners want to like what they like without feeling judged. As much as I dig De La, they could be judgy as hell.

SOMEHOW, *BUHLOONE MINDSTATE* WAS DE LA SOUL'S MOST COMPLICATED AND comprehensive work, a mash-up of funk and soul samples alongside original straight-ahead jazz. It was the second memorable rap album that had a high-profile jazz musician on it, the first being the cornerstone bassist Ron Carter on A Tribe Called Quest's *The Low End Theory*. (Side note: Carter didn't know who Tribe was and only did the session at the behest of his son. Then he listened to the music and wasn't a fan of what he called "objectionable" language. He agreed to the gig after Q-Tip said there'd be no cursing on the song on which Carter was featured, "Verses from the Abstract.") *Buhloone Mindstate* featured the funk and soul jazz saxophonist Maceo Parker on the song "I Be Blowin'," a solo that registered somewhere between the smooth jazz of the '80s and the underground soul jazz of the '70s. De La ceded the floor to Parker's almost five-minute saxophone solo and didn't reemerge vocally until the aforementioned "Ego Trippin' (Part Two)" a track later. This was De La giving flowers to the past and to legends who weren't as well-known. Something rang authentic about it, like they were doing it to give heroes their due, not to grab money. Apparently, if there was dough to be had, De La wasn't getting a cut of it—at least according to Pos's observation. "I am Posdnuos, I be the new generation of slaves," he poignantly declared. "The pile of revenue I create / But I guess I don't get a cut 'cause my rent's a month late."

By '93 and the release of *Buhloone Mindstate*, De La started showing signs of adulthood. They were losing hair (Pos and Maseo, anyway) and started rhyming about topics germane to growing up and settling down. Where other rappers would keep selling misconceptions of overconfidence and financial excess, De La kept it honest. But as much as their fans savored new music from De La, the commercial path ahead wasn't so assured. There was genuine worry within the camp; while *De La Soul Is Dead* sold well, peaking at No. 26 on the US Billboard 200 and No. 24 on the Top R&B/Hip-Hop albums chart, it didn't sell as well as *3 Feet High and Rising*. Artists seeing their commercial impact dwindle can't help but wonder if the end is near or how long they can survive on creative cachet and critical goodwill. And with the changing tide in rap, coupled with infighting among the Native Tongues, residual disdain for Tommy Boy Records, and real-world responsibilities, De La wondered if the ride was coming to an end already. They didn't know if they had what it took to keep blowing up, or at the very least keep it interesting. It's like my good friend and author Jason Reynolds once told me: when you're a noted artist of any discipline, you have to keep pulling rabbits out of hats, yet the hats keep getting smaller. De La extracted rabbits on the first two albums; they were expected to do the same on *Buhloone Mindstate* under incredible pressure. Listeners didn't care or know about the odds they were facing; they knew there was a new De La album in stores and hoped it was jammin'.

Across culture, onlookers love to say that art was ahead of its time as a way to justify tepid responses to it. Somehow, this art is so advanced and forward-looking that it skates modern comprehension and lands in the future—five, ten, twenty years into unknown space and time. But *Buhloone Mindstate* actually was ahead of the curve. Dudes that young had no business rapping about kids and childhoods and personal evolutions. Guys still within college age weren't supposed to sound that mature. We marveled at Stevie Wonder the same way:

no way a kid in his early twenties could make such sophisticated work as *Music of My Mind, Talking Book,* and *Innervisions*. When you look back on the music as an adult, you're floored by its maturity, how it taps into feelings and struggles you don't experience until your thirties. *Buhloone Mindstate* was foundational work for a rapper like Phonte, who in the mid-2000s earned his name by doing the same grown-man rap that De La perfected in '93. The same goes for the rappers billy woods and Elucid, who, under the name Armand Hammer, rhyme about gentrification and their place within rap music as guys in their mid-forties. *Buhloone* embodied the reflection you feel when the late-night partying suddenly isn't so cool, and eating food served from behind a bulletproof shield at two in the morning doesn't feel like the move. The album exemplified awakening, of coming of age in the truest sense.

In De La's quest to blow up and not go pop, as inferred from the album's intro, they presented their most honest work, a searing and sometimes uncomfortable look inside the messy inconstancy of life as adults and famous people. It was also an indictment of the very notion of crossing over, which, for Black music, means being accepted by white audiences. That Black music can't survive on its own without the cosigns of white-run institutions has long been a point of contention, going back to Elvis Presley repurposing the rock and blues of Chuck Berry, Little Richard, and B. B. King and touring it through the Jim Crow South. As the thinking goes, when white people like something, they steal it and act like it was always theirs. That's why on "Patti Dooke," we hear a clip from the film *The Five Heartbeats* voicing how many artists felt. "Why are niggas always crossing over, huh? They can accept our music as long as they can't see our faces?" "Tell me somethin'," that same person declared later. "How come they never cross over to us, huh?" The truth is, we're always expected to come around to what broader culture is doing, not the other way around.

Buhloone Mindstate pushed against this, a compulsion partially driven by rappers themselves. In '94, for instance, members of Wu-Tang Clan could be seen rapping over a pitch-black piano loop in an ad for St. Ides malt liquor. Yet the seeds of this crossover were being planted in the '80s and early '90s. The Fat Boys were cast in Hollywood films. In '91, Digital Underground had a star turn in the horror comedy film *Nothing but Trouble. Buhloone Mindstate* arrived just before hip-hop and pop became synonymous. And because De La had already seen the highest peaks of the industry, their music was, in a way, warning others about what could happen to them. Blowing up wasn't all it was cracked up to be. "We had been through the 'machine,'" Dave once said. "I think we were truly burnt out." In typical De La fashion, they weren't just gonna say no to pop culture; they scrutinized and made fun of it, almost to say that if you wanted this for yourself, you were wack too.

No matter the flashy headlines this person and that person received, De La and others like them were the benchmark of cool in hip-hop, the paragon of regular, purveyors of the mundane. I don't mean "mundane" in a negative sense. Acts like De La were far more relatable than some buff dude in a bucket hat. Surely the Tupacs and the LLs were just as important to the culture, but they shouldn't overshadow De La's common-man aesthetic. The aforementioned artists were cool as hell and we wanted to be like them too. Yet we were more likely to land closer to De La's ground game than LL's all-world aura. To put it in sports terms, De La was Stephen Curry before he was even alive. Though LeBron James gets the rightful pub as the league's top player, no one could rally a crowd like Steph. A three-pointer from thirty feet riled fans more than an LBJ dunk, mostly because we identified with him more: Steph was a skinny 6'3" and Lebron a stout 6'9". Steph looked like the fans who cheered him on, which made him a darling to those in the Bay Area (where he played) and beyond. We loved De La because they never took themselves too seriously, never too distant and not above it all.

It's that warmth that kept De La relevant, along with a brazen ingenuity that never felt over our heads. While eschewing industry norms and disavowing the white cosign, they doubled down on their brand of hip-hop. This approach made people like me believe we weren't so weird or square for liking art that's a little off. I didn't feel like an outsider or unworthy of inclusion.

Buhloone Mindstate was released right as I was headed to middle school and not looking forward to it. Somehow, perhaps because I've always been an old soul, I connected with that album's maturity more than I connected with the first two albums' lightheartedness. Their peril felt aligned with the peril I felt at the time as a teen growing up fast. I was the youngest of my siblings and one of the youngest in my cousin group. It seemed everyone around me was an adult or about to become one, and they were gonna discuss adult things regardless of me sitting in the room. That sort of upbringing can make you feel alone and misunderstood, even more so if you're not into the same things they are. As much as I cherished my upbringing, it was also peppered with moments of solitude, which I tried to assuage with music. *Buhloone* was a salve, its kaleidoscopic score resembling the underground jazz records I learned to love as an adult.

It was much like Miles Davis's 1970 album *Bitches Brew*, an expansive recording full of edgy guitar riffs, plugged-in trumpet wails, and long-winded grooves, a revolutionary record through which Miles shifted the course of jazz once more (the first being 1959's *Kind of Blue*, where he prioritized improvisation over rigid songwriting with prescribed chord changes). Critics panned the album because they didn't understand it. It wasn't what they were used to from Miles. Stanley Crouch, in particular, chided *Bitches Brew* and its predecessor, 1969's *In a Silent Way*, as a maudlin sound in which Miles seemed lost among electronic instruments. It "was little more than droning wallpaper music," he said of *Silent Way*. Of *Bitches Brew*, he said, Miles "was firmly on the path of the sellout. . . . [His] music became progressively trendy and dismal, as did his attire; at one point in the early 1970s, with his wraparound dark glasses and his puffed shoulders, the erstwhile master of cool looked like an extra from a science fiction B-movie." Yet *Bitches Brew* was light-years beyond what other musicians not named Sun Ra were on to back then. The same went for De La from '89 to '91, and held true in '93. Compared with A Tribe Called Quest and Gang Starr, who sampled more traditional jazz in their work, *Buhloone Mindstate* was spiraling and psychedelic, almost spinning out of control yet somehow staying the course.

To achieve this, the guys got back to "buggin' out," as they called it, a term used to describe the band's all-in, every-sound-but-the-kitchen-sink style of song creation. While they bugged out a little—"Breakadawn" combined the opening chords of Michael Jackson's "I Can't Help It" with a vocal loop from Smokey Robinson's "Quiet Storm"—the results were more streamlined and palatable than what transpired on the band's first two albums. They also went to Japan and experienced rap music they didn't understand, taking in the energy of the performances and internalizing them for their own work. They "felt a flow," Dave remembered, "not knowing what they were saying, what they were talking about, but felt the energy." It's why they recorded the song "Long Island Wildin'" for the album, a track featuring Japanese rappers Takagi Kan and Scha Dara Parr, which threw fans for a loop. It certainly threw me for one. International hip-hop wasn't a thing yet, so it was wild to click play on a song with that title and hear a different language. Decades later, bloggers would proclaim it De La's worst song ever, but this was the band buggin' out in the grandest way possible. To my ear, it recalled the ill-fated "Transmitting Live from Mars" and its French spoken word. "Long Island Wildin'" was De La giving their audience a perspective they didn't know they needed, and taking the plunge because it felt right.

Buhloone peaked at No. 40 on the Billboard 200 chart, giving De La the coolest album reception yet. Compare that to Tribe's *Midnight Marauders*: it peaked at No. 8 on the same chart. De La didn't really know how poorly *Buhloone Mindstate* performed until they opened for Tribe and saw the reaction *Midnight Marauders* received compared with their album. It "wasn't really doing what we needed it to do," Pos would say later. "We had this album that wasn't doing well and a lot of different music was changing." After the tour with Tribe ended and it was time to construct another album, "we were just a little disillusioned" and didn't know what to do. The other albums elicited almost immediate acclaim, but this one took a while to catch fire. Critics were mixed, too: In an October 1993 review, the esteemed critic Greg Tate wrote in the *New York Times* that "the easy-listening veneer of *Buhloone Mind State* may please those who thought that De La Soul needed to come down off the high horse it rode on *De La Soul Is Dead*. Stauncher fans may wonder if *Buhloone Mind State* doesn't mark a retreat from the dizzying expressionism of the group's earlier work." In *Entertainment Weekly*, the writer James Bernard took the opposite approach. While he thought *De La Soul Is Dead* was "sprawling and unfocused," he praised *Buhloone Mindstate*'s concentration. He wrote: "Unhampered by the countless skits that the group laced between the songs of their previous albums, *Buhloone* is more economical—its beats are simple, but the tracks are alive with intricate layering and small touches that make them undeniably catchy: soul samples and jazzy notes over rolling bass lines." The group itself noticed a slower burn following the album's release. Across several interviews, Pos has mentioned how fans didn't connect with the album until years later: "They'd say, 'I didn't really get it.' You know, but, 'When I had my first kid,' or 'When I got a little older' . . . 'When I went back to that album, it really appealed to me more than when it first came out.'"

Buhloone Mindstate dropped two months before three historic albums would see the light of day: *Midnight Marauders* and Wu-Tang Clan's *Enter the Wu-Tang (36 Chambers)* on November 9, and Snoop Doggy Dogg's *Doggystyle* later that month—on the twenty-third. Tribe was already a household name at that time, and that album didn't disappoint. In fact, in rankings of the group's albums, *Midnight Marauders* is often considered the best. *Enter the Wu-Tang* and *Doggystyle* were highly anticipated debuts: The Wu had generated a buzz behind the singles "Protect Ya Neck" and "Method Man" and would break through early the following year thanks to the monumental track "C.R.E.A.M.," which cemented the group as an industry powerhouse for the next decade. *Doggystyle* introduced Snoop as a transcendent talent. *Buhloone Mindstate* got lost in the shuffle of those records. In the case of the Wu, their album—with its muffled drums, lo-fi sampling, and muddy mixing—ushered in a dirty sound that birthed groups like Odd Future in the mid-2000s and an offshoot from that crew, the rapper/producer Earl Sweatshirt, in the mid-2010s. Meanwhile, Snoop's album helped keep the focus out west, a run that began with his mentor Dr. Dre's solo album *The Chronic* in '92. The East and West Coasts would soon battle for the figurative title of best rap, and albums like these—along with the Notorious B.I.G.'s *Ready to Die* and Nas's *Illmatic* in '94—kept the tug-of-war going until the late '90s. *Buhloone Mindstate* wasn't considered a linchpin; it was in the middle of the pack.

Where the allure of albums like *The Chronic* and *Doggystyle* has dissipated as the tolerance for misogyny in hip-hop has waned, the light surrounding *Buhloone Mindstate* has only brightened—for me especially. In middle school, I didn't know who I was or what I wanted to be. I still didn't fit in with the cool kids, but I wasn't a nerd either. My voice was changing, I was getting taller, and my clothing choices were trash. Party shirts, jeans that weren't baggy enough, Timberland work boots (the ones with the bolt on the side and not the tree), and the one burgundy polo shirt I wore entirely too much. To quote regional slang, I was a bamma. *Buhloone Mindstate* arrived at a transitional moment in my life. As a hip-hop head, I had—and loved—all the cassettes I mentioned in the paragraph above. But none of them spoke to me the way De La did on *Buhloone Mindstate*. It felt familiar, lived-in, complex but simple, psychedelic, and forthright. I dug *3 Feet High* and *De La Soul Is Dead* and can understand why listeners hold those two in higher esteem, but *Buhloone* resonated at a time when my musical psyche and mental constitution were developing in tandem. Even if Dave himself didn't like the album—"I think we were just a little too creative," he once said—it's refreshing to listen to it today and hear rappers who gave a damn about the craft, not just the veneer of rap stardom. I appreciate an act like De La Soul because, if nothing else, you knew that each project would be different with a whole new set of worldviews to pick apart. And by the time *Buhloone Mindstate* came around, De La wasn't in a laughing mood. Neither was I.

What they were trying to do musically started to make sense, thus dictating the left-leaning, off-kilter work I'd champion throughout my career. In my weird little way, I sometimes felt these artists needed an ally, someone who came from that same community and had a platform to tell the world about it. Not that De La ever needed a megaphone, but I was protective of them and their contributions. It's why we rallied when the record label held their music in limbo and away from digital streaming services. It's why their fans ponied up over six hundred thousand dollars when they announced a Kickstarter campaign to finish recording their 2016 album *and the Anonymous Nobody* . . . . Three albums in, De La had soundtracked my formative years and, for others, their teenage years into adulthood. While older heads could appreciate what they were doing (especially since there was jazz and the lyrics were relatively clean), De La Soul was just as important as any noted act from any corner of the mainstream.

At a time when corporate contracts and bottle popping were on the horizon, they were one of the last vestiges of a free-spirited past that wanted the art to stay how it was. Or to at least evolve within the parameters of the art and community. But like all things, hip-hop culture needed to grow up and show out, and the mid-'90s was that time. De La was walking into a much darker world and didn't like what they saw.

FROM LANDOVER WITH LOVE

6

I N 1995, YOU COULDN'T TELL ME I WASN'T GOING TO BE A PROFESSIONAL rapper. I was a full-on backpacker, going to open mics, spitting bars about anything to anyone who'd listen. I was beginning to notice the so-called underground, aka rap that was just as dope as the mainstream but without a big marketing budget. I thought I identified with that crowd more than the other. FM radio had nuanced playlists that accounted for various forms of Black music. For that reason I still thought the radio was a great place for discovery; that I could hear everything from Biggie Smalls to Black Moon was a win. I rapped because I was a decent writer and thought I had a shot at getting on the very radio I respected. I rapped because De La Soul foresaw where rap music was headed and did their best to steer it left. Where Wu-Tang Clan formed my propensity for lyrically dense rhymes that took years to decode, De La felt more attainable. In turn, me and my fledgling rap group—the Final Chapta—partially fashioned ourselves after them: a colorful hybrid of the Wu and De La that rapped for rapping's sake and looked like everyday students going to public schools in Prince George's County, Maryland.

As the chasm between mainstream and underground began to widen in the mid-'90s, De La Soul presented a curious case: they qualified as both. I've always wondered if, given the chance to recast their career, they would've signed to another label. Or if they'd eschew the label system altogether and sell the music themselves. There wasn't a clear pathway for going indie then, so the prospect of inking a deal with the label that put out Afrika Bambaataa's "Planet Rock" was an attractive one. The push and pull of success always tugged at De La, which cut both ways. As much as any artist says they don't care about numbers, they're still indebted to them to a certain extent. That their sales declined with each album weighed on the band—and in turn the label—and it was something they thought about, regardless of the stance they displayed publicly.

There's an internal evolution with anyone who's found success in a particular field, who's good at that particular thing and doesn't want to keep on keepin' on just because. The reality was that by 1993 or '94 De La had to shake things up in an attempt to stay relevant, and regardless of their wariness toward the machine, they had to play the game too. With progress comes growing pains and strife. By the time *Buhloone Mindstate* came and went, the partnership between De La and Prince Paul splintered. Compared with his involvement on the previous albums, where, as the seasoned producer, he had a bigger hand in driving the music's creative direction, he was pretty much hands-off on *Buhloone Mindstate*, taking more of an adviser's role, making the calls to get legends like Maceo Parker and trombonist Fred Wesley in for recording sessions. Paul was still very much a producer, just in a different way. Pos, Dave, and Maseo had a clear vision and knew what they wanted to convey.

De La was becoming an also-ran, and that didn't sit well with them. Even within their barely-there Native Tongues collective, the adoration they once received was now going to their peers, namely Tribe. That put De La in a weird space: the same groups they opened the door for were now getting the bulk of the goodwill. Times were changing, they were changing, and the public appetite for their music was changing. Even the recording process was changing. "It wasn't laughing the whole time," Prince Paul said of the *Buhloone Mindstate* sessions. "We were seriously making a record." By Paul's own admission, the guys were becoming more thoughtful and less whimsical. They were growing into adulthood, and Paul's ideas were still somewhat juvenile. That's not to say De La wanted to be overly deliberate, but Paul once had them make sex sounds in the recording booth to simulate an orgy; the band was now (and probably then) way too old for that kinda shit. "What I brought to the band they might've outgrew," Paul admitted.

Buhloone Mindstate was the most confounding album they'd released (the horns and the vocals were centered in ways that other rap albums hadn't achieved). That, to me, is a good thing. A little hiss adds texture to the recording. It makes the music feel lived in, comfortable, nostalgic, and lends to the long-term appeal of the release. There's nothing wrong with a little dirt in the mix. Paul was a hot commodity in music production who leaned briefly into making horror-themed beats—on the album *Horror City*—before getting back into comedy-centered music and long-form storytelling. By the late '90s, Paul released the albums *So . . . How's Your Girl?* as one half of the group Handsome Boy Modeling School and the solo *A Prince Among Thieves* to critical acclaim.

It's always better to end things too early than too late, and it was good that Prince Paul and De La split when they did. We don't have to look far to see other examples of hanging on too long: by the time Tribe's fifth studio album, *The Love Movement*, was released in 1998, it was clear that Q-Tip and Phife Dawg weren't cool with each other, and the record suffered as a result. Conversely, after the release of *Buhloone*, De La—and rap music in general—was headed for the "keep it real" era, a high-stakes civil war between mainstream and underground, authentic and fake, those doing it for monetary excess versus those doing it for the culture. While such divisions existed prior to the early to mid-'90s, they only ratcheted up once more eyes were fixed on them.

While De La was in the lab piecing together what would be their next album, acts like Biggie and Snoop became icons. You also had groups like Mobb Deep and Onyx, alongside acts like MC Eiht and Cypress Hill, all of whom skewed decadent in their own ways, but with a darker, brooding slant that spoke to the seediness of street-level crime and weed consumption. Even my faves were doing it. I remember going up for Redman's *Dare Iz a Darkside*, which played like a warped, psychedelic trek through the darkest recesses of mental instability exacerbated by heavy drug usage. When you go back and listen to it, Red is basically talking about weed and sex the entire time, despite its engaging nature. It was of the same ilk as De La, a bugged-out record leaning into absurdity as a form of sonic liberation. This is what the band brought to hip-hop, an unabashed sense of place and perspective in a genre teeming with characters. But De La still felt underrated. It always seemed they were whispered about while others got overwhelming praise.

Many underground and unheralded artists have complained about the same occurrence, that despite real ones knowing what they bring to the game, there's a tendency to forsake what's dissimilar. It's human nature to take consistency for granted, and De La Soul was remarkably consistent. Still, they were always going to have a tough time with this newer, darker blend of rap music, because it just wasn't them. But to De La's credit, they never tried to make it theirs, even if it meant selling fewer records. Rappers like Redman kept De La's essence alive even when they didn't have a new album out, which was the greatest compliment to a trio that sometimes felt left behind. But what I didn't realize was that De La were adept beatmakers on their own, that beneath the "eh, whatever" facade was the intensity to win—for themselves and their young children. I also think that's an underrated aspect of De La's impact: they presented themselves as middle-class guys who seemed perfectly fine with an OK existence. That they could pay their bills and provide for their families was the most important; the prospect of rap superstardom—and all the industry bullshit that comes with it—didn't seem as attractive.

But here's the thing about middle-class living: You're neither rich nor poor. You're just sorta there, and that can get old too. You can see fame and notoriety just around the corner and failure just behind you. Either option is scary; as much as we trumpet a life without financial stress, the pressure to always deliver is a prison within itself. No one wants to be just *OK*, so to navigate a place in between brings a different set of challenges. The push and pull fosters comfort and unease, a mix of keep on keepin' on with the desire to break through fully. People also can't understand when you're cool with being leisurely, when you're not overly driven by the same desires as everyone else. Thus the dilemma of De La Soul in the mid-'90s, a band in the middle of the road that was losing ground fast.

By this time, Tommy Boy was preoccupied with their other acts. When De La signed, they didn't have as much on the roster. So there was more investment in De La's success because, well, the label needed it just as much as the group. For a company that began as an incubator for electro-funk breakbeats, signing De La meant tapping into a new audience. Tommy Boy was the house that De

La built, whether or not the label owners wanted to recognize it. As a result, they made Tommy Boy a destination for other artists who may have taken their talents elsewhere—artists like Queen Latifah, House of Pain, Coolio, Digital Underground, Naughty by Nature, and a young, unproven drag queen and singer named RuPaul. These artists each had chart-topping hits, so while the label still appreciated De La artistically, they weren't only looking to them to help keep the lights on. That cut two ways for the group: On one end, a robust roster meant they were free to create however they wanted, without the need for a radio hit. On the other, with the label not paying them as much attention, they couldn't help but feel forgotten or not as loved as before. In De La's heart of hearts, it was still *Eff Tommy, they did me dirty!*, but there was still something weird about seeing their labelmates getting the adoration they used to receive. Regardless, their flop records were still going gold.

As they were raising kids, going on tour, and creating music in silence, I found myself getting deeper into Tribe and Gang Starr, as well as the solo projects the Wu released. I was getting into jazz thanks to Tribe's work, even if I couldn't fully articulate what hit so hard about those acoustic arrangements. Indirectly, it opened me up to new sounds and ideas and forced me to reckon with other genres of music to inform my own songwriting. But I was thirteen. By then I was struggling academically, and I didn't think I would get better. My mother, aunt, cousins, and grandmother would all try to talk with me, but I simply couldn't see my worth. I just didn't care about grades or anything that wasn't music.

Some would say it's a part of growing up, but I legit didn't feel like I belonged anywhere, a feeling I still wrestle with today. Alongside Redman's *Darkside* sat Raekwon's debut album, *Only Built 4 Cuban Linx*, a gritty seventy-minute conceptual piece about dealing cocaine with some fashion talk in between. Then there was Onyx, three bald guys from Queens who rapped like they'd shoot you in the face just because it's Tuesday. I would never blame rap music for societal ills—I'll leave that to older, out-of-touch politicians—but I believe you can tell a lot about a person by the art they consume. And if you were to raid my cassette cases, you'd find a kid who didn't really care about life or people or the future. I just wanted to rap, play basketball and video games, and read liner notes. I didn't realize until years later that De La taught me to be positive, to lean into my varied emotions, to be myself and not care about anyone else's opinion. That's also something I wrestle with to this day. I'm still fighting to live in the present.

IN 1994, POS, DAVE, AND MASEO SAT ON A COUCH IN A STUDIO IN LOWER Manhattan, fielding questions from Fab 5 Freddy on *Yo! MTV Raps*. It was a chill-enough scene, the fellas decked out in '90s finery with baggy jeans, big shirts, and floppy hats, playing *Super Mario Bros.* on Super Nintendo. There wasn't anything remarkable about what was happening, but this was the coolest thing ever. You mean De La likes video games too? It was flawed thinking, of course—adults like video games just like kids do—but to see major rap stars being portrayed as regular was truly inspiring. They didn't have to be extravagant to be seen. Back to Eddie: Before him, Black actors in cop movies had to be transcendent. Either they were literally saving white people or they were breaking down racial walls through teachable moments that led to some sort of aha kumbaya crescendo near the film's end. Or, like in the blaxploitation era, they were ultra-heroic, sliding across car hoods, running through burning buildings, catching all the pimps and low-level street pawns in an attempt to clean up the ghetto. They had to be visible, be enormous, be masculine. They were representing their entire race. Eddie was different: in 1984's *Beverly Hills Cop*, he came off as just a guy who happened to have a gun and a badge, who was trying to solve his friend's murder but could maybe steal a car if the situation called for it. At no point did he present himself as some paragon of Blackness that was trying to uphold the weight of his people. Instead, he was just Axel Foley, a dude from Detroit driving a crappy blue Chevy Nova, proving himself smarter than a Beverly Hills Police Department that did everything by the book. The role was revolutionary. It showed that Black people can exist without having to be outstanding.

De La wasn't exceptional because they were ordinary; they were an exceptional group that happened to be ordinary. In the 2020s, ordinary became the wave. Someone like Black Thought, the lead rapper of the Roots, enjoyed the solo notoriety he was due in the '90s. Back when albums like *illadelph halflife* and *Things Fall Apart* were being released, he was considered a sharp yet unshowy rapper without much sizzle. As of this writing, billy woods—a Washington, DC–born rapper partially raised in Zimbabwe— might be the most popular underground MC in the world. He's an incisive scribe with an expert eye for detail; where others would describe the hospital and stop there, he describes the snacks in the machine, evoking a stronger sense of place in his work. Quelle Chris is an Oscar- and Grammy-nominated artist whose style as a producer and rapper leans into the same sort of comic absurdity as De La. In each instance, the artist wasn't over-the-top remarkable; instead, their skills did the talking. Even as they were onstage or spitting conversational bars about life in South Philly, sneaking liquor into the club, or sex as exercise, respectively, they drew direct lines to De La's nonchalance about structure and rules. So while their interview with Freddy wasn't especially groundbreaking, at least optically, their exuberant joy was refreshing, especially at a time when such light was frowned upon. They weren't selling the Black trauma porn that greenlights TV shows and books and gets top billing on bestseller lists.

By 1994, the violence that permeated hip-hop was getting out of control. Six years prior, before De La released their debut album, a series of violent incidents erupted during rap concerts at the group's hometown Nassau Coliseum, which led to promoters banning such shows at the venue. This led to conversations about violence in hip-hop and whether or not rap music was good for the public. Because rap was still seen as a fad and not valued as art, the incidents made it easier for those who didn't like rap in the first place to blame the entire genre for a smattering of occurrences. Never mind that violent incidents had also stemmed from heavy metal concerts. That same year, Nelson George, then *Billboard*'s Black music editor, coordinated with Jive Records executive Ann Carli and rapper KRS-One to record a one-off track featuring rap music's biggest stars to take a stand against the bad press and to show the rest of the world that hip-hop culture wasn't negative. Released in January 1989, "Self Destruction" featured KRS, members of Stetsasonic and Public Enemy, Doug E. Fresh, MC Lyte, and Kool Moe Dee, among others, and it presented a united front against what felt like a tidal wave of opposition to hip-hop culture.

Gun violence had dire consequences in 1994 when Tupac was shot five times outside the Quad studio in Times Square by an assailant self-identified as Dexter Isaac. He and two other men made off with forty-five thousand dollars in jewelry. The twenty-three-year-old Tupac had been in court the previous day to face allegations of sexual assault. The shooting and robbery happened as Tupac entered the building's lobby and was headed upstairs to record a verse for the rapper Little Shawn. Reportedly, Lil Cease—a friend of the Notorious B.I.G.—called Pac up to the eighth floor. When he entered the building, Pac was struck in the hand, head, and groin and was carried upstairs to the studio, where police were called and the rapper was taken to the hospital. Pac blamed B.I.G. and the record mogul Sean "Puffy" Combs, claiming they knew about the robbery ahead of time. Then B.I.G. dropped a song called "Who Shot Ya?," a single B-side not included on his recently released album *Ready to Die*, which prompted Pac to think the track was about him.

Then B.I.G. and Pac started beefing, and then the East and West Coasts started beefing. At the Source Awards in New York's Paramount Theater, the Atlanta rap group OutKast got booed, and Death Row Records CEO Suge Knight took a verbal shot at Puffy during the ceremony. Puffy and B.I.G. introduced a glossier strain of rap with decadent imagery that prioritized the same celebratory lifestyle that De La mocked in the "Ego Trippin'" video. Using well-known soul and funk samples, Puff and B.I.G. made it cool to pop bottles in the club's VIP section, to live an easy life and not fear that it'll vanish. Being Black and successful in the United States means thinking prosperity is somehow a lie. There's a feeling that the other shoe will drop soon, and that all the cars and clothes along with that big house will be taken back soon enough. Musically Puff nudged rap out of its scarcity mindset. Put on that suit, he urged. Stunt on these folks like you belong here too. His perspective had value, but back then he was considered the poster boy for selling out. Underground rappers and "real hip-hop" lyricists thought he symbolized what was going wrong in rap music, that the art of hip-hop culture was slowly giving in to monetary excess. Puff also brought an either-or aspect to the game. If you didn't like him, you were a "hater." The term eliminates any sort of nuanced criticism; not every negative comment is rooted in jealousy.

B.I.G. had more creative currency. As the crown jewel of Puff's Bad Boy Records, he had a big hand in the stuntification of hip-hop—with his tailored suits and Versace shades—but the man could rap his ass off. Be it street rhymes or flossed-out flows, B.I.G. sounded natural both ways and was one of the rare MCs who garnered respect from the mainstream and the underground. Also coming up was a young rapper from Bed-Stuy, Brooklyn, named Jay-Z, who also shared Puff's ostentatious sensibility and B.I.G.'s approach to freestyle lyricism. In

1996, he would release his debut album, *Reasonable Doubt*, a flashy, semiautobiographical coming-of-age tale about his ascension from dealing drugs in the New York area to becoming a young mogul in the making. In the coming years, he'd wade deeper into mainstream rap, eschewing street narratives for glossy pop hits. Jay would be seen as part of the problem with '90s hip-hop culture as well. Here was another dude who could actually rap choosing to create pop-adjacent music to keep selling millions of records. No one could blame him for that, but in a culture quickly running out of allies, the underground was falling behind the mainstream.

This era was lambasted for embodying everything that was wrong in hip-hop. But because Jay-Z's records sold millions of copies, rappers looking to cash in followed the trend. Before long, even tried-and-true lyricists like Nas and Kool G Rap were changing their images, ditching the hoodies and baseball hats for fancy suits and mafioso personas. Sometimes it worked: Nas's *It Was Written* was actually a decent album that didn't deserve all the backlash it received (because it wasn't *Illmatic*, his landmark debut LP). Yet for the most part, the shiny-suit era was a dark time. Never before had the culture been so divided. And never before had it been so perilous. It felt like someone was going to die from all this, and with positive role models like the ones featured on "Self Destruction" off doing other ventures, I wondered if there was anyone who cared enough to squash the beef and restore order.

I'm not saying hip-hop was supposed to return to what it was in the '80s. Music and culture of any kind are supposed to grow and evolve and morph into new forms of creativity. But the balance that once typified rap was slowly giving way to uniformity. The business of rap was taking over, and this transformation signaled the end for the Native Tongues movement. For listeners increasingly enthralled by crime-centered songs, the idea of leaning into serenity and upliftment didn't seem so enticing.

Dave saw what was happening and didn't like it. "In order to be cool, enjoy life and be somebody—you've got to be in the music business," he once said. "It's so sad that you can't escape it." When he went to clubs, he continued, "everybody is coming up to me trying to be a writer, a production supervisor or something. It's not about lovin' life, being happy and enjoying. It's about being a rapper and being in the entertainment business." To him, the bureaucracy behind the music made it less enjoyable. Everyone was entitled. No one came out to shows unless there was some sort of check attached. It was no longer about supporting the art or even checking out something new and challenging. Everyone wanted to be seen, to be the loudest voice in the room, to hold court. "It's so tired," he concluded. "Talent, art, and intelligence are no longer concerns."

For Maseo, at least, rap should've stayed rap. R&B should've stayed its own thing too. Hip-hop-inspired beats with scratches and hard drums were being used in soul music. It resembled rap without being called rap. Such developments rubbed MCs the wrong way, because it was yet another example of executives and producers cashing in on rap without giving the genre its proper respect. In what's sadly still a practice today, execs associate with the genre because it's cool. They like the money it generates, the fashion, and the slang, but they don't fool with the music itself or the Black people making it. Instead of coming up with original music, Maseo argued, they threw sampled rap underneath the singer and kept it moving. "It's wack," he said, "so they needed a beat to get over with."

I'm floored by the hypocrisy in that statement; De La's biggest song was a simple loop of a Funkadelic track. Though the guys were supreme lyricists and Mase a standout DJ, one can't ignore that part of the appeal of "Me Myself and I" was the beat. That it sampled such a well-known band only helped De La's popularity, and to forget that they were once upstart musicians trying to make it was a disservice to newer R&B acts. The notion that they could sample songs in the name of rap but others couldn't felt misguided and out of touch. These new kids didn't care as much and didn't understand what made De La Soul important. Surely they were around during De La's heyday, but songs like "Change in Speak" and "A Roller Skating Jam Named 'Saturdays'" didn't hit them as hard. They didn't have the same context and thus couldn't grasp why folks went up for the band at all. When compared with what was popular at the time, De La Soul might've seemed a little too alternative for Pac and B.I.G. loyalists.

Dismayed, De La started crafting their first album without Prince Paul. *Stakes Is High*, in 1996, was a treatise on the state of hip-hop and the group itself. This was their *What's Going On* or *There's a Riot Goin' On*, a survey of what was happening artistically and not liking the view. Like the Marvin Gaye and Sly and the Family Stone albums, there was love within the margins, a glance at the past, but it took hip-hop culture to task in clear, plainspoken language. Or at least as clear as De La was going to be at any point. And where *Buhloone Mindstate* was mostly the result of Pos's creative vision, *Stakes Is High* was largely a Dave record. It's where he took a major step forward as a beatmaker and producer, and where the trio collectively (then in their upper twenties) noticed they were now the "old guys" in the club, so to speak. The competition was fierce because the industry was so saturated. De La wasn't singular anymore; other like-minded acts were making similar music and garnering good press too. De La had to shake up their sound and try to compete in a space where the public's attention was divided. Even Tommy Boy Records, which had been an indie label, was thinking about expansion. They had a partnership with Warner Bros. Records, releasing certain projects through a joint venture.

Shaking up the sound meant staying in the studio, learning how to use new production equipment, and being foremost in the sonic creation of the LP. They'd always been hands-on with the making of their music, but for now, Prince Paul wasn't there to be the safety net. If listeners didn't like *Stakes*, it was on them. "Taking the seat of being the producers of this record was fun, sitting down and actually putting our heads together and putting beats together solely was really cool," Dave said. "It did make a very important statement even for what we [were] feeling at that time with our turning point," Maseo continued. "Are we still going to exist here?"

In any instance, the shortest route is a straight line, to attack the situation head-on with direct action. Dave would set a strong tone for this on the album's title track, a mission statement for the entire LP. In his opening salvo, the second verse after Pos, he took aim at Puff, hard-rock street dudes, the rap-R&B hybrid, and the Source Awards. "I'm sick of bitches shakin' asses," he proclaimed. "I'm sick of talkin' about blunts, sick of Versace glasses." And so on and so forth: he hated slang, half-assed award shows, name-brand clothes.

I was sick of all that shit too. Not because the perspective wasn't viable but because it became the way to succeed, and all the big names followed the blueprint. Everyone had the Hype Williams–directed video with the bikini-clad dancers in it. And everyone had either the tailored suit and cigar or black hoodies and gold teeth and shot dice on the street. I didn't see anyone who looked like me. No regular folks doing regular things. Hip-hop didn't pay much attention to those between the margins. You had to be either-or: flashy or ashy, glossy or abrasive.

The video for "Stakes Is High" was an act of revolution. In it, Dave is doing laundry while running down mainstream Black music. He isn't doing any of the usual stuff you see in rap videos. He is just being Dave, throwing clothes from the dryer to the table, rapping to the camera and to an audience member on an imagined episode of *Maury*. For the album overall, the group wanted to show that the true secret to keeping it real is staying true to yourself. If you're a hard-rock dude, cool, be a hard-rock dude. If you're uptight or knew the steps to the Urkel Dance, that's fine as well. Happiness and acceptance were De La's greatest contributions, so on the title track when Dave said, "Smiling in public is against the law, 'cause love don't get you through life no more," he was lamenting days gone by when everyday life wasn't so heavy, when one could encourage others and not be labeled soft. Then as always, De La challenged archaic tropes of what it meant to be a man in rap music. There's nothing weak about honoring others or admitting that you're hurt or struggling and need help.

De La opened *Stakes Is High* with an appreciation of Boogie Down Productions' debut studio album, 1987's *Criminal Minded*, which introduced us to the producer Scott La Rock and the battle-ready lyricist KRS-One, whose diss to the Queens-based MC Shan on "The Bridge Is Over" was one of hip-hop's first highly publicized battles. But it's not one of the first albums brought up when discussing the greatest rap albums ever, so De La gave it flowers instead. De La's shout—through a cavalcade of voices—made me revisit the album and understand why De La acknowledged it at all. It's not just one of the first gangsta rap albums ever created; it showcased KRS-One's ability to tell a robust story. That BDP posed with weapons on the cover proved influential to N.W.A, who released the breakthrough *Straight Outta Compton* and became megastars a year later. But the groundwork was laid by Boogie Down, and then inspired De La.

De La doing that on their second straight make-or-break album crystallized the we-don't-give-a-fuck-ness of the Long Island band, which endeared them to BDP and purehearted rap fans who openly supported the culture. "We were just trying to think about, 'How can we start *Stakes Is High*?'" Pos remembered. "We [were] like, 'Yo, let's try to do a collage of just people saying stuff.' I just left a message on my phone and whoever would call I was like, 'Yo, just let me know the first time you heard *Criminal Minded*.' Everyone just started leaving messages and telling me when they heard it." Simple enough, but effective.

The first time I heard *Stakes Is High*, I was in my aunt's townhome once again, this time as a fifteen-year-old sitting in the basement, spinning the CD in a black boombox I'd gotten for Christmas. Before I pressed play, I was trying to write a rhyme, just scribbling a free-form thing that never quite materialized. As usual, I was trying to be opaque, something about quasars or whatever, because I didn't know how to tell a story or write a song. I didn't have many life experiences. I hadn't dealt with rogue police officers or experienced romantic heartbreak. Those occurrences would come just a few years later. So I didn't have a well to draw from. But when the murky clatter of the intro track came rushing through, then the cavernous stomp of "Supa Emcees," it locked in right away that this was a different De La and that the best way to write is candidly. I remember being challenged by the album in the same way I was challenged by the earlier ones. But this one was disarming, complex in its simplicity. Where I was prepared to hear something wild on the previous records, the blunt force of *Stakes Is High* presented its own challenge, almost a dare to say your feelings with your chest. Let the rest be what it is. I put down my pen and let the music run its course. Then I approached my artistry with new eyes.

After the final note of the album closer "Sunshine" ascended into light, I devoted myself to new ways of conveyance. Lines about space gave way to rhymes about my maternal grandmother's fight against cancer, her endurance as a loving woman who fought to shield her family from harm, and what I perceived was a wanting to reunite with her husband—my granddad—in heaven. A lot of days, I could tell that my grandmother wasn't doing well, but I couldn't quite articulate my inner workings. She was always there, making biscuits and watching her stories, giving me a stern word when I deserved it. So I wrote a verse called "A Better Place" that I never performed;

instead, I took it to school and let some friends read it. Like Pos and Dave in their early days, I was apprehensive about rapping publicly. I was too self-conscious and unprepared for whatever ridicule I might receive. I also didn't want to face the fact that my grandmother was dying and I was devastated. I was lost and couldn't fathom what was happening to her. For whatever reason, I don't remember much about my grandfather's transition. I was shielded from it. Though I knew he was sick, he dealt with it quietly, shuttling back and forth to doctor's appointments while still finding time to watch baseball, drive me to school, and shoot balled-up notebook paper into the trash like a basketball. My grandfather epitomized silent dignity; his noble passage was what he preferred.

De La helped me cope with confusion, grief, and the feeling of loss. I say "the feeling of" because I believe those loved ones never left; they're here spiritually. The group offered a healing sound, a friendly voice in my ear. They weren't doing anything over-the-top by then; they were just there, and sometimes that's all you need. De La was like that old friend you haven't spoken to in years, yet the conversation never falters, no matter how long the silence. They were there telling me it was OK, that it was fine to sit with sadness as long as I channeled it into something heartfelt. Eventually the pain subsided and wasn't so stifling. There were still pockets of anguish, but optimism wasn't so distant.

Equally introspective and outward-looking, *Stakes Is High* was a self-assessing take on creative displacement and a brotherly gaze from a band that knew better. On the song "Itsoweezee (Hot)," another Dave standout, the rapper derided the Italian mob cosplay that permeated groups like Wu-Tang Clan and lyricists like Kool G Rap. Even the hook surveyed the state of hip-hop at the time. It lambasted the power that money had over hip-hop culture and the lack of love within it. The video was innocent too: Dave floats throughout a high school as food fights and playground hangouts commence. Several other like-minded rap artists appear in the clip as well: Pharoahe Monch, Monie Love, and Lords of the Underground, among many others. It promoted community, a sense of family within so-called alternative hip-hop. It recalled the early days of De La Soul, before the record deal and the fame, when they were just kids having fun without worldly pressures. No one was a gangster or trying to be one.

But I can't talk too much trash about the aliases or the gangsta rap posturing. I got swept up in it as well. Because I was a Wu fan, I found myself coming up with different names to buttress my rap name, 2781 (my birth date and year), but they weren't based on some gangster I'd never met. As Dave pointed out in the song, Italian mobsters don't even like Black people, so the choice to fashion themselves after that sect never made sense. It didn't make sense to Maseo, either, a Brooklyn native who went to school in Bay Ridge, an overwhelmingly white section of the borough. "It was rough," he said. "I got chased home many times by Italian white boys. I got my ass kicked a couple of times too. It was all part of the premise of just being Black." *Stakes Is High* conveyed a pronounced disappointment in rappers who grew up precariously but forgot where they came from once money entered the picture. And, as Maseo put it, organized crime was different from street crime: "There's certain things that push you to a limit when you're hungry, but that doesn't make you a gangster. Where I'm from, gangster shit is definitely organized crime. Just because you killed somebody don't mean you a gangster."

Regardless, the whole gangster trope had dire consequences. In September of that year, Tupac was wounded in a drive-by shooting in Las Vegas and died from his injuries six days later at the young age of twenty-five. Six months later, B.I.G. was shot and killed at a traffic light in Los Angeles en route to a party in the Hollywood Hills. He was twenty-four. In a short span, a genre that was once celebrated for giving voice to the disenfranchised had two high-profile murders, causing some to wonder what the hell was going on. Those were the darkest days the culture had ever seen. While *Stakes Is High* wasn't meant to solve societal ills, it was designed to deter rappers from a lifestyle that could kill them. It's one thing to be an MC and play gangster; it's something else when an actual gangster tests you. And that's why De La Soul chose to celebrate *Criminal Minded* as a launchpad for *Stakes Is High*: the BDP album set the blueprint for how satire could operate in rap music. By playing the role of a so-called gangsta rapper, KRS—who prided himself on being an educator in hip-hop—was indirectly dissuading peers and casual fans from that sort of life. On *Stakes Is High*, De La adopted a similar ethos, but with a strength they hadn't used before. Avoiding sarcasm, they asked hip-hop a simple question: What the hell is wrong with you?

Around this time, I started falling out of love with it. I didn't feel like hip-hop culture—or, maybe, mainstream hip-hop culture—was for me. The clothing, the sanitized sound, none of it. I'm not knocking anyone who likes high fashion, but I was bouncing between Landover and Suitland in Maryland, and I wasn't gonna hit the local mall and buy expensive brands to stunt for my classmates. In fact, I didn't start buying fly sneakers until I began working at Sears in Landover Mall, and even then I had a cash-only hookup that saved me a few bucks. My friends had similar sensibilities. They also liked alternative hip-hop but could equally appreciate Biggie and Jay-Z. But I felt my ear skewed a little further left than usual. While they're rapping along to Nas, I'm quietly studying the rhythms of Elton John's "Daniel" or David Bowie's "Cygnet Committee." This was the era of big jeans and Eddie Bauer coats, and you couldn't mention Elton and Bowie without people looking at you crazy.

Rocket Man and Ziggy Stardust aside, underground and alternative rappers catered to my personality. Because they didn't care too much about appearances but never looked sloppy. They exuded the type of come-as-you-are vibe I assumed hip-hop was built upon anyway. For the first time, around 1996, what I consumed through

TV and radio didn't feel so healthy—and I didn't feel invited to the same party to which everyone else was invited. So I stopped looking to terrestrial radio for the latest and greatest. I started going to rap shows at the 9:30 Club and to one-off open mics at the old MCI Center. I considered other avenues where curious developments were happening: rap ciphers in my neighborhood, local talent shows, and the Freestyle Union in DC, where noted lyricists like Kokayi, Black Indian, and Toni Blackman were teaching young vocalists how to rhyme off the head. And when I wasn't doing all that, I was listening to *Stakes Is High*, a record that fought to preserve the past while forecasting the future. Change is constant, De La argued, and artists should be adequately compensated for their work. But money doesn't matter without integrity. Don't lose your soul chasing checks.

WHERE WERE YOU THE FIRST TIME YOU HEARD STAKES IS HIGH?

POS AND DAVE MASTERED SLEIGHT-OF-HAND FLOWS THAT SOMETIMES landed them in hot water. Occasionally they were direct, like on "My Brother's a Basehead" and "I Am I Be," but sometimes they could be too slick. So when Pos rapped "Stick to your Naughty by Nature and your cane, 'cause graffiti that I based upon the wax is insane" on *Stakes Is High*, the average listener took it as a diss to the New Jersey rap trio, almost to say: *Listen to them if you want substandard bars; fool with us for the elite ones.* That's how Naughty heard it too. They thought it was a surprise attack from a labelmate. The whole thing felt random; that it appeared right at the top of the album made it feel like an announcement.

Turns out it wasn't a diss at all, according to Pos. "I was just trying to say to someone like, 'Yo, you stick to your way of how you get down," he said. "Because what I have, it'll get you beyond high. I'm just too potent. Instead of this saying, 'You'll stick to your nature because you can't deal with my nature,' I just said 'Naughty by Nature,' it sounded dope to say, kind of just playing on words. If someone was like, 'I come sweeter than Jeru.' I don't think Jeru [the Damaja] would have been like, 'Yo, you nicer than me?'"

I don't buy that. If a rapper said something like "I got more soul than De La," I'm guessing Pos, Dave, and Maseo would've taken issue with it. So I'm not surprised that Naughty felt a way about the line, as no one from the outside looking in would be able to discern Pos's wordplay in the split second it took for him to say the rhyme. Quite frankly, it felt like a callout, even if he said he didn't mean it that way.

The challenge with some artfully inclined rappers is that they expect listeners to comprehend their intent, even if the lyrics are convoluted and intricate and the meaning is buried too deep to be deciphered. There's some backstory happening that doesn't quite connect, or the lyrics only make sense when recited backward on a hill at dusk. As much as I identify with alternative hip-hop, I've also encountered rappers online who take issue with their music being misinterpreted by writers and casual listeners. Sometimes artists (myself included) can be too cryptic or highbrow. They can be a lot like certain jazz scholars who lambast those who don't know every Duke Ellington deep cut and can't tell them exactly how many footsteps there are between the Blue Note and the Village Vanguard. If the message didn't land the way it was intended, did it really land at all?

After hearing the rhyme, Treach, the co-leading rapper of Naughty by Nature, was disheartened by what he perceived to be a diss. The groups were cool with each other because De La let Naughty open for them early in their career. Treach was surprised that De La would diss them, because he loved them. It also felt out of character for a group like De La, who prided themselves on being fans of other artists, to suddenly start taking shots at their peers. They usually only attacked when they were attacked.

Not thinking the line was anything serious, De La went about their business like everything was fine, figuring the two sides would talk it out eventually. Naughty rapper Vincent "Vin Rock" Brown called Pos to clear the air, then Treach approached Maseo about it at a music seminar. At no point did the group foresee the misunderstanding becoming physical. But it did one night in New York City in 1996 when, during a show at the Palladium in Times Square, a crowd of rambunctious patrons tried to pull Pos off the stage. Turns out those were Treach's associates, and Treach himself even tried to get in on the fight at the show. "There was definitely a misunderstanding that turned into a rift," Maseo recalled. "Everybody is a little sensitive and insecure about a whole lot. He feels like he's got to do something about it because his crew is saying one thing and the record really means something else. That was a time in rap where there was a lot of pop shots being taken and given all across the board throughout the entire genre."

Stakes Is High was released to mixed reviews and didn't make much commercial noise. *Rolling Stone* gave it two out of five stars and chastised the group for not returning to the bright psychedelics of *3 Feet High and Rising* or the dark satire of *De La Soul Is Dead*. "While the luscious, Curtis Mayfield–inspired 'Sunshine' soars mightily, most of the 17 pieces on *Stakes Is High* crawl along life-lessly, trailing a wake of assembly-line beats that impart all the ex-hilaration of a suburban traffic jam," David Sprague wrote in his critique. Calling it "cranky," *SPIN* writer Jeff Salamon said *Stakes Is High* was a missed opportunity for De La to release another left-field masterpiece. "Though the wordplay is typically sharp and elusive on

Stakes, De La's musical chops have gone by the wayside," he wrote. "There's a not-unpleasing nimbleness about *Stakes*, but toying with a groove, not merely establishing it, has always been the appeal of a De La record." *Entertainment Weekly* gave it a B, a high grade considering the criticisms in the review. "Hip-hop's trippiest trio take an unfortunate turn for the conservative on *Stakes Is High*," writer Ethan Smith observed. "Musically, they've traded in their gorgeously weird jazz-based soundscapes for sparser, straight-ahead beats. And while they've always had a cynical streak, Posdnuos, Trugoy, and Maseo now frequently verge on utter joylessness."

Nostalgia can be powerful, tricking us into believing that something is better than it is. Oftentimes, people my age defend '90s hip-hop as the golden era, acting as if nothing bad ever came from the time period. It's the same reason why fellow graybeards got upset when the rapper Vince Staples downplayed the decade, and why some older heads didn't rock with Odd Future in the 2010s. The future is scary, and it's even scarier for them when they don't see themselves in it. And when some kid comes along emulating the past, sometimes exceeding it, it can feel like an attack on the youth they still covet. Older music reminds them of passing time, when their parents were younger or still alive, when they were spry or athletic, when opportunities were infinite. As you get older, you become more invisible, a little lonelier. Not everything ages well, and I'm here to tell you: we had some bricks come out in the '90s; don't get it twisted.

Stakes Is High wasn't one of them, though. That the album was chastised, in part, because it wasn't De La of the past is the same sort of misguided thinking that befalls a lot of critics, myself included when I first started reviewing music. The critics didn't like *Stakes* because they wanted it to be something else. They forgot that artists are supposed to evolve from song to song, project to project, and can't play the same notes they used to. Are you the same person you were last year? Five years ago? Ten years ago? Then how can you ask others to tread the same ground repeatedly? Yet we do it all the time, to upstarts and legends alike, expecting them to stay where we want them to preserve our own youth. *Stakes Is High* De La was never supposed to sound like *3 Feet High* De La or *De La Soul Is Dead* De La. How did critics expect dudes in their mid-twenties to sound like dudes in their teens? If writers didn't like *Stakes* on its own merits, cool, but so much of the criticism reads like the effects of OD nostalgia from people who never wanted De La to grow in the first place. The same type of critic shuns Stevie Wonder's *Journey Through the Secret Life of Plants* because it wasn't *Songs in the Key of Life*. Or John Coltrane's *Ascension* because it wasn't *Giant Steps*. It's the critic's job to assess what's there, not what isn't.

Stakes Is High was released in the summer of 1996 amid the wave of the Fugees, an enterprising new group out of New Jersey akin to the Native Tongues, but with more dynamism. In the group was the rapper/singer Lauryn Hill, by far the crew's biggest star, a generational rapper and singer. In February of that year, the Fugees released their sophomore album, *The Score*, a multifaceted collage of rap, reggae, and R&B, powered by the singles "Fu-Gee-La" and "Killing Me Softly," a remake of Roberta Flack's song from 1973. The album, with all its critical acclaim, ushered in a new vision of the Native Tongues, grander than what De La, the JBs, and Tribe would have imagined. *The Score* became a global phenomenon, selling more than seven million units in the US and five million in the UK.

Also in '96, good-to-great albums like Busta Rhymes's *The Coming*, Jay-Z's *Reasonable Doubt*, Nas's *It Was Written*, and A Tribe Called Quest's *Beats, Rhymes and Life* were released near De La's, and the group had to fight for attention in a crowded landscape. Yet *Stakes Is High* didn't seem designed for immediate acceptance. While the album had anthems, it was just gonna hang around—the time signatures, the one-liners, those would be picked apart for years to come. It was a time capsule and a slap in the face. "I get tired of certain MCs getting considered dope MCs, and I know I'm saying something," Pos once said of the record's intent.

Where others heard despondency, I heard rejuvenation. Most importantly, I heard fun. Not funny accents and make-believe sex orgies in the studio or children getting bullied in the schoolyard, but fun in a grown-up sense. The kind of fun you have as an adult in house parties and speakeasies, where the laughs come just as fervently, this time over brown liquor with close friends. *Stakes Is High* wasn't joyless; it just wasn't juvenile. It also introduced us to a young lyricist from Bed-Stuy named Dante Smith, who performed music and acted under the name Mos Def, and catapulted a Chicago rapper named Common to greater recognition. De La had been the barometer for all things young and hip; now, as elder statesmen in the industry, they needed new inspiration to keep their music vigorous.

Mos was a guiding force throughout the album, offering his memory of *Criminal Minded* in the intro (he first heard it in the Roosevelt Projects), shooting dice at the beginning of the title track, and featuring on the deep cut "Big Brother Beat." He was in the rap group Medina Green, but anyone who heard him knew he was destined for solo stardom. Mos was that magnetic. *Stakes Is High* gave him a platform to rap with one of the most heralded groups ever, which, in turn, nudged Pos to improve lyrically. Common had already garnered attention three years prior with his sophomore album, *Resurrection*, a sleeper hit powered by the still-profound "I Used to Love H.E.R.," a love letter to hip-hop culture. While Mos and Com saw this as a learning opportunity, Pos saw it as a step toward the future, a passing of the baton, so to speak. Mos went on to release my favorite rap album of all time in 1999, *Black on Both Sides*, a comprehensive record of Afrobeat, soul, and funk that scanned as hip-hop but wasn't solely indebted to it. The album wouldn't exist without the example that De La set forth and the platform they afforded Mos on *Stakes Is High*.

Though they were perpetual students, De La underrated themselves as they got older, almost to the detriment of their legacy. Maybe they played themselves down by being a little too laid-back. In whatever era of hip-hop, the biggest stars were always superhero types who forced you to reckon with their sound. De La never did that and was taken for granted as the years went on. Their lack of assertiveness led to people overlooking them as a good-to-pretty-good group that didn't really command your attention. The members of De La have recorded solo material and guested on other work, but their friendship always brought them back to the unit. Their lyrical synergy was so tightly wound that solo albums likely wouldn't have had the same impact. Some listeners don't rate Pos and Dave as dope MCs individually because they've always operated within the De La universe. It would have been bigger news if they split up or spit bad verses (they never did). While Pos, Dave, and Maseo surely had disagreements, they learned to accept each other as they were, never letting singular quirks get in the way. "We've been blessed to be three individuals who don't let ego run who we are as individuals," Pos once told the *Daily Beast*. "We can do things without each other but it's with the respect and the support of the other members."

Every so often, no matter the industry, you have to stand up for yourself and let people know just how dope you are. It isn't bragging if it's the truth. Though they helped launch the careers of countless artists, including Mos, Com, Dilla, and Tribe, it felt as if these acts passed them by to a certain extent. No one really gives credit to the innovator, and not enough people have given proper credit to De La Soul as conduits to the next generation. As much as they innovated and inspired, I have a hard time reconciling why there wasn't more public chest-thumping about them until Dave passed. Was it because they were too nice? Were they the victims of rapidly changing interests and shifting tides in the music industry? I don't know.

As time passed, however, you'd hear the guys doing more features outside of their own work. I remember when I heard Pos and Dave on "Gettin' Down at the Amphitheater," a funk-centered gem on Common's 1997 album *One Day It'll All Make Sense*. Then there was the album *Uptown Saturday Night* from the New York duo named Camp Lo, a record that I slept on initially before my classmates told me how good it was. Dave appeared on the track "B-Side to Hollywood," a lighthearted tune on which he rapped about disparate topics: Saturday morning cartoons, breakfast cereal, Popeye, and his favorite month of the calendar year (it's June). In 1998, De La Soul brought their coolheaded humor to the double-disc *Lyricist Lounge, Volume One*, a compilation of underground and mainstream rap songs featuring Mos and Common alongside the experimental poet Saul Williams, KRS-One, and the Philadelphia rapper Bahamadia. With these artists, though, De La simply cracked jokes as if to simulate an open-mic format, and it sounded like Pos and Dave were truly in their element—laughing, smiling, and talking about nothing to kill time before the next act came on (or, in this case, before the next song played). It was joyful, and, most importantly, they sounded comfortable. Almost like those kids from '89 talking about fish and whatnot.

Quietly, De La reassembled their own vision of what a Native Tongues collective could look like in the '90s with younger, fresher MCs who were just kids when the first iteration took shape. De La's vision of the future lived within the music of the aforementioned artists, and I could see why the group, as Pos did on the *Stakes Is High* title track, declared the Native Tongues "reinstated." Once again, like they'd always done, De La found a way to hang around and shift culture. "They're a platinum-status group," DJ Premier once told me. "They still have not strayed away from their wordplay and style. Why change what makes you great? Your style of greatness should always be present in anything you do, no matter what the year is."

I've been around long enough to see this happen: Every few years or so, the so-called avant-garde becomes the old guard, and the music that some would call eccentric is suddenly the standard-bearer for what pushes the culture forward. Somebody like André 3000 can come back seventeen years after OutKast released their last album, release an LP of ambient flute-driven meditative music, and have listeners reconsider the subgenre after years of it existing underground. The same for Kendrick Lamar in 2015: his second studio album, *To Pimp a Butterfly*, which featured some of the best jazz musicians in LA, opened the door for the genre to become popular in the mainstream marketplace once again. We owe a great debt to De La. Even as the Fugees' *The Score* earned its rightful respect, that too was a testament to the examples set by Pos, Dave, and Maseo in the previous decade. But memories are short, and the fellas struggled to maintain their status as headlining performers, despite their legend. Yet to Premier's point, De La was still the standard-bearer for how to sustain yourself in hip-hop and not lose your soul along the way.

They proved that staying the course is the best route. Trends fade away, but good work doesn't. The world will discover it in time. In an industry full of new artists and new songs to consider, listeners always come back to the classics. And this may sound like a cliche, but it's true: consumers have deeper connections with good people, or at least people they perceive to be good. It's possible to thrive on your own terms and not be awful. At times when it seemed their legacy would be lost, life always seemed to fall into place for De La, their honesty never going out of style in an era when the facade was paramount. It's better to last forever than exist for a minute. De La played the long game.

I've always considered *Stakes Is High* a companion piece to *De La Soul Is Dead*. Beyond the black and gray hues covering the respective album jackets, both projects harbored a sense of mourning—of past selves and old ways. On *Dead*, Dave's dreadlocks were "heading out the door," as he put it, and the members had to kill themselves to stay alive, their figurative death a way to reset expectations. The mourning in '91 was the mourning of creative freedom and anonymity, a longing for the days when their whereabouts weren't so scrutinized and going to the mall just to kick it was a good Saturday. *Stakes Is High* asserts the band's independence after years of attachment to Prince Paul. While it mourned or, perhaps, wished for the downfall of gangsta rap, and the subgenre of new jack swing, with its upbeat electronic drums and dance-oriented R&B-meets-rap groove, *Stakes Is High* had similar smoke for the things hampering the culture they once loved wholeheartedly—a blunt object swung wildly. It's also my favorite De La album. It arrived during a period of pronounced self-actualization, when I had the clearest perspective yet on who I was. For the first time, I had confidence as a creator and a student, and I developed friendships that still endure to this day. The lyrics on *Stakes Is High* hit me hardest because I understood them the best. Where *Buhloone* helped me develop musically, *Stakes* had rhymes on it that I still recite. Whether I'm walking around the neighborhood or driving through my hometown, the album takes me right back to my sophomore year of high school, even though I'm not trying to relive my youth.

In therapy, you're encouraged to let go of your past self en route to a breakthrough. To live in yesteryear is to linger on situations you hoped happened differently, or those that you wish to relive. Indeed, it takes a strong will to let go of what no longer serves you—whether positive or negative. The glory and struggles of history can weigh you down if you summon them too often. In music, it can be even tougher to move on if your past work was impactful, especially if you're signed to a major record label. Yet De La mastered the shedding of creative skin for the sake of long-term vitality. I've seen artists put out the same music over and over, only to wonder how they lost the joy of artistic creation. The sales quietly diminish, the nominations dry up, and the concerts don't sell out.

I'm not saying De La was the first act to eschew caution and come with new sounds for each album (Stevie Wonder says hello), but they were one of the first in rap to blatantly ignore the machine to salvage their own peace of mind. I've always appreciated Common because, from 1994 to 2005, across a catalog that includes noted albums like *Electric Circus* and *Be*, you were guaranteed to hear some new shift from project to project. *Like Water for Chocolate* was informed by neo-soul and Fela Kuti's Afrobeat, and the aforementioned *Circus* was a psych-rock-infused project inspired by Jimi Hendrix and Pink Floyd. This held true for all the Soulquarians: Erykah Badu, D'Angelo, the Roots, and so on. No two albums sounded alike, a tactic inspired by De La. I can also look around the current landscape, to rappers like Kendrick and Vince Staples as harboring the same courage.

I know what it's like to be pressured into your past self. You're essentially playing into someone else's vision of you, and that's always a recipe for failure. You'll never be able to live up to how others perceive you, and some already have a preconceived notion of your work anyway, so it's best to ignore public discourse and do what you feel. Still, in those quiet moments of dissension, it's easy to doubt your vision and be fearful of how others will receive it. That's human nature; in our heart of hearts, we all want to be loved and accepted, and for several thousand strangers to fawn over what we put into the world. There's nothing wrong with feeling that way; especially during the Covid-19 pandemic, when we were all shuttered at home and the isolation felt especially crippling, many of us wanted to feel some sort of connection to the outside. And if you were a creative type, you either sat with the despair of the time or let it push you toward some sort of great unknown. Greatness, or, at the very least, freedom, resides in that unknown. The uncertainty of doing something different that the audience may not understand outweighs the comfort of doing the same ol' same. De La are the poster children for not giving a damn. You can love, like, shrug at, or dislike the records, but they've always challenged listeners to come around to what they were doing. There was likely something in there to hold your attention, something you couldn't quite figure out but that was worthy of the journey.

I didn't know it at the time, but *Stakes Is High* would be the last album of De La's golden era. As much as I liked the LP, there was also a somber aspect to it, a feeling that rap music was going to keep changing in a way that might not leave room for De La. Never before had critics reacted so coldly to their perspective, so eager to diminish their sound in favor of something another act was doing. De La had always signaled the way forward; suddenly, it was written as if they were the ones playing catch-up. Even their friends labored in this new reality. The dynamics were changing.

Neither Tribe nor De La likely wanted to admit it, but their albums were always in competition. So in '96, either at the lunch table, on the phone, or on the bus, the question was this: *Stakes Is High* or *Beats, Rhymes and Life*? When asked the equivalent query three years prior, when *Buhloone Mindstate* and *Midnight Marauders* were released in the same year, the overwhelming favorite was *Midnight Marauders*. It fused jazz and rap the best. But this time, with Tribe on the outs and *Beats* sounding unfocused, the clear answer was *Stakes*. De La still presented a unified sound; Tribe not so much.

ONE DAY IN THE SPRING OF 2023, MY NEIGHBOR ASKED ME IF BLACK PEOPLE still had struggles. I looked at him strangely, let a smile form on my face, then responded with just one word: "Absolutely." He asked because he'd been looking at old videos of the poet Amiri Baraka on YouTube and was listening to *Stakes Is High* on his boombox. During his lifetime, Baraka wanted liberation for Black people and envisioned a separate Black nation where our kind could truly be free.

My neighbor was taken by one line in particular, delivered by Pos on the title track: "Our skin not considered equal / A meteor has more right than my people." The line, he said, held special resonance with him as a former rapper who was trying to find some level of truth in his life and career. It was also foreign to him, since he never considered De La much of a political group. But when you listened to them, they had these brief moments of social commentary, lines cut through because they weren't expected.

Pos's rhyme channeled an old Gil Scott-Heron poem called "Whitey on the Moon" that took America to task for caring more about space travel than equal rights for Black people. The Vietnam War was underway, protests raged throughout the United States, and the fight for civil rights reached a fever pitch. On his poem, Scott-Heron sounded exasperated, laughing between the lines almost to say, "All this is happening on Earth, but you would rather turn your attention to Mars." It *was* laughable, the foolishness of it: in a country built on the backs of Black folks, the leaders would rather look away from their fight and toward the cosmos. Pos's line reimagined Scott-Heron in a way. Here we were in '96, almost thirty years after his composition, and we were still fighting the same issues we always had. A big rock hurtling through space had more rights than Black people.

And that's what my neighbor was taken by, the honesty that landed with a thud. Pos wasn't breaking any news, but he and De La had this remarkable way of cutting through the din with one-liners that just sort of struck out of nowhere. My neighbor is around the same age as De La and is connected to the group in ways that are beyond my own connections. To him, they were fellow New Yorkers who'd done good, no different from a neighbor or friend who made it out the neighborhood. To him as a rapper with far less fanfare but with an album selling for hundreds of dollars on the vinyl marketplace Discogs, their ascendancy and prolonged relevance gave him hope that he still mattered—that being in his fifties didn't mean he had to go somewhere, sit down, and remain out of sight. The rhyme is almost thirty years old and still hits with the same force that it did when he first heard it.

This is the same neighbor who could tell I was mourning Dave's death and saw that I needed some sort of reprieve from the dark cloud that followed me in his passing. My neighbor's observations about De La helped me remember that being political doesn't just mean shouting down government officials or storming the streets with a bullhorn and bad intent. Divergence is its own form of protest. Saying what you mean in the face of opposition is its own form of protest. Telling the truth is protest. In an industry that prioritizes window dressing, speaking up for your people doesn't go out of style.

It wasn't until later that I thought about it, but we as socially conscious people were also protesting the status quo in my high school. It wasn't so much of a hard stance; we were just trying to fit in as best as possible. It's tough to see yourself as some sort of revolutionary when you're sitting at the cool-enough table and your place in the world hasn't been solidified yet. My neighbor grew up the same way. He'd talk about his days at a rigorous high school in Brooklyn, being pulled between two worlds as a smart kid growing up in Fort Greene when it wasn't so popular.

He also fell victim to the tired hip-hop trope of Black hip-hop kids having to dumb themselves down or toughen themselves up to make it home without a fight. My neighbor was weird like I was weird, like Janelle Monáe and Tyler, the Creator, were weird. So De La spoke to him the same way they spoke to me. He's ten years older with different lived experiences, and here we are connected by music and upbringings, standing on a sidewalk in a gentrified neighborhood, trying to parse one seismic line spoken by Pos. Then, as it always did, De La's message unified.

Though Black Americans have—and, sadly, will always have—struggles, somehow De La brought a comfort that made my neighbor feel seen, that made me feel seen, that made millions of others feel seen. Nowadays, my neighbor sits outside, weathered from years of trying to exist as a Black man in this country, playing the music of his youth for passersby. Sometimes he'll play Ultramagnetic MCs or Grandmaster Flash and the Furious Five. Other times it's jazz or easy listening. It almost always comes with a quiz: "Hey, Flav" (he calls me that because he says I've got soul), "you know who that is?" When he plays De La, stopping me as I walk back into the building, we both let out a "yooo" and keep it moving. No other words are exchanged, just a quick handshake and gestures of peace. We both know what it is: De La is the end-all be-all.

Everyone from my aunts to my cousins understood De La, even if they couldn't explain what it was they liked about the music. De La has always been around me and my family, soundtracking discovery. That De La was just there and I can't exactly remember how they arrived pretty much speaks to why we're here, right? Regardless, I've always felt that by the mid-'90s De La fans had to work a little harder to defend the group. In the late '80s, when the goodwill was paramount, it was easy to categorize their work as buoyant and playful. But in the *Stakes Is High* era, when put up against actual dark records, it played like Onyx, Wu-Tang, or Mobb Deep lite. Why listen to the so-called hippy dudes when you can play *All We Got Iz Us* or *Hell on Earth*? The community around De La was beginning to shrink, and the group almost came off as an underground act that only a few heads knew about. Don't believe me? Listen to Pos. "I made girls' brown eyes blue at will," he said on "Wonce Again Long Island" from the album, "until my ass was no longer mass appeal."

To that end, I can't help but fixate on Pos's visceral reaction to his peers in the mid-'90s. The sheer frustration in his voice when talking to *Rap City*, the look of consternation on his face, the push and pull of honesty and diplomacy in the way he spoke. In one quote, told to Joe Clair in an interview, he expressed anger about the way he's viewed as an MC. It was the first time I remember seeing Pos feel a way about being underrated. It's not like he was wrong, but in years past—at least publicly—he would've shrugged it off and just kept making the music he'd always made. My ear fixates on the song "Long Island Degrees," where Dave took aim at the Notorious B.I.G.'s mental state. "I got questions about your life if you're so ready to die," he said, referencing the Brooklyn MC's debut album *Ready to Die*. What happened to the love, the excitement, the bliss?

De La disappeared after the release of *Stakes Is High* and stayed out of sight until the turn of the millennium. There was no grand reason for why they left. It was just time to revisit the drawing board and start working on the next album. In their absence, hip-hop became even more commercialized, a lot chillier. It wasn't until recently that some critics decided they pegged the album all wrong. Twenty years later, after the allure of the shiny-suit era wore off, they realized—as *Slate* put it—that the LP was one of "concern rather than conservatism, walking a tightrope between the productive uses of history and the simplistic allures of nostalgia."

Even now as I revisit *Stakes Is High*, I wrestle with the same nostalgia referenced in the *Slate* review. In '96, as I struggled with the passing of my grandfather and the gradual passing of my grandmother, there was something comforting about listening to three dudes trying to reconcile their emotions for public consumption. Even as I struggle with pronounced grief following the recent passing of my mother, the album feels like a balm in this time of uncertainty. Not that the group said anything on the LP directly related to death, but it reminds me of days gone by, when she would take interest in the music I liked, even if it didn't speak to her. She encouraged me to listen to De La. She liked the bass line on Nas's "Shootouts," the timbre of Mos Def's voice on his late-'90s work, the soul sample on Ghostface Killah's

"Camay." She didn't dig the lyrics, but she didn't police my absorption of them. As I play *Stakes Is High* in 2023, the visions come rushing back. I see us in that old house in Landover, me in the back room hunched over a boombox. Most importantly, I see her. I hear her. I appreciate her willingness to let me rap, to let me run the streets with my friends and collaborators Troy and Thomas while still keeping a close eye on my movements. My love of hip-hop largely comes from her, simply because she let me explore records like *Stakes*. The album still feels like a private conversation in hushed tones.

When my grandmother passed in '97 and I had to navigate without one of my greatest protectors, I found myself listening to De La–adjacent rappers, reveling in the same poetry. A year later, Mos Def and the Brooklyn rapper Talib Kweli formed the duo Black Star and released their debut album, *Mos Def & Talib Kweli Are Black Star*, to decent fanfare. I went up for that record, not just because it was dope but because it was the closest thing to De La— and, in turn, my family—that I could hold on to at the time. In hindsight, it's easy to look back and wonder why people didn't like mid-'90s De La. But they meant something different to me. They helped me through the roughest parts of my life, connecting me to the past and reminding me to lean on love. In grief, sadness can quickly grow to anger. Tears turn to clenched fists and notions that you have nothing to lose. De La was medicinal, the reset I needed and still need.

LIFE WITHOUT DE LA

THE RZA, ON THE INTRO TO THE SECOND DISC OF WU-TANG CLAN'S HIGHLY anticipated sophomore album *Wu-Tang Forever*, made a statement with resounding impact: "This ain't no R&B with a wack nigga taking the loop," he said audaciously. "This is MCing right here. This is hip-hop." It was ironic coming from the Wu-Tang leader. As much as he wanted to think that his group was still the underdog, they were more establishment than underground, a battle the crew endured over its next few albums. There were differences brewing between acts like the Wu and De La and Puffy and his Bad Boy empire. De La was partially to blame. Though they voiced how their peers felt about sanitized blends of rap, they were one of the bigger names to voice this displeasure, which had more bite than some unknown disgruntled rapper taking shots at the Bad Boy throne. In a 1998 article for *LA Weekly*, the writer Miles Marshall Lewis pointed to a De La show as a flash point in the battle between so-called real and mainstream rap music.

At the Tramps nightclub in Manhattan, he witnessed fans booing the rappers Lil Kim and Foxy Brown, which might speak more to hip-hop's misogyny than to the fight between disparate factions of hip-hop. To this day, sadly, women who rhyme still get an inordinate amount of vitriol from hypocritical men who rap about sexuality but suddenly have a problem when women do the same. On this night, Kim and Foxy reportedly caught the ire of underground rap fans who were tired of their kind—rappers who flaunted their wealth in the music and supposedly didn't take the art of rapping seriously. Nonetheless, a new crop of young lyricists were making their way through hip-hop—rappers like the Yonkers-born fire-breather DMX and the Bronx-bred Big Pun, brash collectives like the Master P–led No Limit Records and the emergence of the Dungeon Family in the South (an all-star squad featuring OutKast, Goodie Mob, and the production unit Organized Noize).

For the first time ever—and I can't believe I'm typing this—I wasn't even thinking about De La. There were too many other dope rappers to choose from. Rappers like Lauryn, who in '98 released her meteoric solo debut album *The Miseducation of Lauryn Hill* and became one of the biggest artists on the planet. And lyricists like Big Pun, whose first album, *Capital Punishment*, was also quite forceful. With tongue-twisting flows and battle-ready bravado, he was seen as the newest hybrid of underground and mainstream rap, an undeniable presence with superstar appeal who could spit with the best of them.

With the release of their respective albums *Vol. 2 . . . Hard Knock Life* and *Aquemini*, Jay-Z and OutKast continued their ascent to the top of the genre, one a future billionaire and arguable Greatest Rapper of All Time, the other a group in Southern rap that broke the mold for hip-hop experimentation in pop culture. I dug all these artists, though my sound palate started broadening. My best friend, Brian, introduced me to the political rock band Rage Against the Machine. Rage, to put it plainly, was De La Soul on creative steroids—a tour de force of rap and psychedelic rock that couldn't be categorized by music media. Through their lead vocalist, Zack de la Rocha, you could hear a deference to De La and the Native Tongues, but also Boogie Down Productions and Public Enemy. They were the gateway to experimental music that went deeper than De La, even if the Long Island trio attuned my ear to inventive sound in the first place. Rage gave voice to the anger I felt, the angst of being rational when life was irrational. They seethed and stomped, forcefully nudging listeners to look at global atrocities and do something about them.

I knew that De La's time was passing, or maybe *pausing*. I was a teenager and firmly entrenched in alt-music scenes throughout the DC area, some of which didn't involve rap or anything near it. I met lifelong friends in high school and others who introduced me to the very artists I salute through this book. De La was still the pinnacle, but I wasn't beholden to them like I once was. I was still rapping with my own group. We did local talent shows and I briefly considered a career as a full-time rapper. I never could freestyle, though. In the '90s, if you couldn't rap off the top of your head, your career was pretty much DOA. So I started leaning into writing as a career path, with journalism as the anchor. My yearbook teacher Carol Kilby suggested I apply for the Washington Association of Black Journalists' Urban Journalism Workshop. Every weekend, on campus at Howard University, I learned how to write articles and speak to strangers on the street. My academic and creative paths were overlapping. Without my favorite group releasing albums and with other younger, more inspired artists taking up the room typically reserved for De La, I debated the worthiness of Eminem and the grandeur of Busta Rhymes's first three albums (Was the world really gonna end with the year 2000?) while digging properly into R&B.

When I was eighteen, my mother's former colleague gifted me a copy of Stevie Wonder's four-album greatest hits CD *At the Close of a Century*. I knew about Stevie, of course, but I only knew the hits. It wasn't until I studied the compilation and purchased his '70s albums individually that I realized two things: some of his B-sides are better than the hits ("Joy Inside My Tears," anyone?), and he wouldn't be held captive by anyone else's perception—not even Berry Gordy's. As for the Lenny Kravitz phase, songs like "Are You Gonna Go My Way" and "Circus" dominated my headphones and the speakers of my mom's Toyota Corolla en route to the basketball court. Then one evening, I walked downstairs and saw this old Clint Eastwood film on TV called *Play Misty for Me*. There was a beach montage featuring this voice I'd never heard singing a slow, romantic ballad. The song was "The First Time Ever I Saw Your Face" by Roberta Flack, the Virginia-born, DC-based producer, vocalist, and arranger. The timbre was so angelic that the rabbit hole only deepened: Roberta led me to Donny Hathaway; Lenny led me to the Beatles; Stevie led me to Herbie Hancock, which led me down the pathway of jazz.

I was in the midst of a transition. As a junior in high school, suddenly everything I did affected my academic future, and I wasn't ready for another part of my life to be that heavy. Advanced Placement classes, weekend journalism workshops, and the everyday rigors of the college-bound course load made everything feel serious. Slowly, I was becoming an adult—albeit a young and naive one—and didn't have as much time to consume music. I eventually stopped rapping: between missed studio dates and the lack of collective interest in practicing for shows, I quit the group to focus on journalism, which I believed was the gateway to a life of professional scribbling. I was becoming a fully realized human being with joy, doubts, and fears; sometimes that took precedence over an evening playing rap CDs and memorizing Cappadonna's verse on "Winter Warz." Also the mainstream stuff wasn't as good, at least not to my ear. The rap being spoon-fed to us in the late '90s was too clean, too much like pop, and too tailored for nightclubs with bottle service. There shouldn't have been such a class division between the underground and mainstream, but there it was, plain as day, seemingly in perpetuity, with the type of rap I preferred being relegated to late-night radio, poetry slams, and mid-size performance venues. I took time to get my future together, to find out what topics beyond music excited me as much.

De La Soul was doing the same thing; they were pretty quiet in the years following their fourth studio album. They would do shows here and there, yet for the most part the guys were taking time to live life and focus on things that mattered long-term: family, real friendships, rest. For a band that lived their lives on the road and in recording studios, staying home and raising kids was certainly quite different. "We really don't have a fear of that 'out of sight, out of mind' thing," Dave once said. "It gave us the opportunity to stay home and really focus on family." After eight years of the same routine—record an album, tour, record another album, tour—Pos, Dave, and Maseo needed a break from the conveyor belt. There was more to life than just rhymes and beats.

While away from the limelight, De La recorded three albums that they wanted to release as a single project, though just from the sheer volume of music, it would be impossible to do so. Those albums, three installments of a series called Art Official Intelligence, each had different themes but were meant to hang together as a sonic representation of the three members. As it were, the AOI records were supposed to state the creative intent of Pos, Dave, and Maseo through retro-futuristic beats and imagery indebted to the type of early-'80s electro-funk that pioneered hip-hop. This was to be another example of the music that De La longed for, but with a throwback look that sidestepped the fashion of late-'90s pop culture. Was it based in the present? Sure. De La was still competitive and fighting to exist in a game they helped create.

But even the notion of "real hip-hop" feels myopic in the greater discussion of hip-hop as a whole. To say the music is either real or fake based on your own preference does more to segregate the art form than to unite it, and it fosters resentment within the audience it's supposed to serve. The idea that hip-hop isn't real unless it upholds '80s and early to mid-'90s ideals ignores all the great hip-hop that came after it. Just because it came in a different package, in the triplet flow of Atlanta's Migos or the sex-positive rhymes of the Bronx-raised Cardi B, didn't make it any less formidable. Still, every so often, someone dismisses newer hip-hop because they don't think it's as technically sound. Such thinking is rooted in insecurity and fear—fear that younger rappers won't defer to the pioneers like they're supposed to, fear that the older heads are becoming irrelevant. With each passing generation comes the possibility of being lost to time. Those most scared of fading away are the ones who never really evolved, who spit the same raps or make the same pop without taking any creative risks. The notion of safety permeates the music industry, the idea that the sonic left turn won't be embraced by listeners. So certain artists and executives encourage the same music repeatedly to keep the gravy train rolling, to keep Spotify streams up, to keep this and that person paid. The listener suffers in the end; the art gets stale, becoming white noise after a while.

To counter such mediocrity, De La kept reconstructing their image without regard to their place in the canon. With the AOI series, they killed everything—the PR, the label speak, the perceptions of who they were and what they represented—and began anew. The first album, 2000's *Art Official Intelligence: Mosaic Thump*, in particular, was meant to be a club record (or as club as De La could go) with booming drums and darting synths akin to what you'd hear in after-hours venues. Some said it was like *3 Feet High and Rising*. It was a good time for the sake of a good time, and that resonated with listeners who clamored for the band's older days. "*Mosaic Thump* is definitely a chorus-driven record with a party vibe," Dave said then. "Not like Jay-Z or DMX, but an enjoyable, sing-along record that you can really get into, poppin' while you're throwing a cool little shindig at the house and everybody's just listening to the good vibes." It was like soundtracking a party with the game's most intriguing rappers: Redman, Busta Rhymes, Xzibit, Tash, and Freddie Foxxx. You're having a good time, but there are still bars to absorb, messages to adhere to, jokes to laugh at. It was the first album since *3 Feet High* without baggage.

De La had the type of renewed spirit that only comes from time spent away from work. As a teenager, I didn't understand this. Why would an artist need to disappear? How can you replace the thrill of recording and releasing music and having thousands of strangers scream along with the words they know? The record deal and all that time on the road—that's gotta be cool, right? Unabashed fans tend to act this way, myself included at the time. We think the artists belong to us, then feel some type of way when we find they're human beings who need to chill sometimes. But it wasn't until I started talking to artists off the record and onstage that I understood their insecurities and self-doubts. While we see them on red carpets, they're still worried about paying bills and creating art that'll be broadly accepted. They want to create unique work that encourages others to create unique work. They want to be seen and appreciated for who they really are, not who managers and label execs want them to be. Back then, I was totally culpable: My faves couldn't stray too far from their popular records; just make *Stakes Is High* or *Black on Both Sides* again.

About Mos: While I liked *Black*'s 2004 follow-up, *The New Danger*, it just didn't have the same communal essence as the previous LP. *Black on Both Sides* was the breezy album you walked around Fort Greene with on some cliche shit; *The New Danger*, with its emphasis on grunge rock and bedroom soul—courtesy of his band, Black Jack Johnson, and the producer Minnesota— was the album you played while stomping through dirty snow in boots you don't care about. It wasn't until I started creating my own work that I realized how much artistry is dictated by real-life circumstances—not some romantic peril that you write about, per se, but the mundane that has nothing to do with the work itself. It's in those moments that creativity happens, when you stare at the ocean or fold clothes, when you speak with a neighbor or watch a film you wouldn't normally check out. Art happens when you slow down and let life happen, when you allow those nuances to push you elsewhere. As your mind eases into rest, it allows new ideas to flow through. It's why De La dipped, why Mos took his time, why artists like D'Angelo, Sade, Maxwell, and Rihanna take forever to release new music. No matter your place on the creative spectrum, you draw from an empty well after some time, and you can't refill it by simply doing more work. Now, as I write articles, liner notes, and this thing you're reading, I also struggle with the real and the arbitrary, the actual world and the imagined one where art is manifested. It's tough to pull creativity from nowhere, to suppress pressure and live while keeping burdens at bay.

What keeps you going when, despite your best efforts, interest in your work seems to wane? With contemporaries like A Tribe Called Quest and EPMD disbanded, De La kept pushing along, proving that groups can stay together through creative differences. Somehow, the group has been able to evade the artistic pitfalls that have befallen numerous acts before and after them. I think De La has persevered because neither MC was drastically better than the other, even though they were both exceptional. Pos's flow was complex yet conversational, full of potent one-liners that came through in rhythmic waves. There was a syncopation to it, as if his cadence operated as another layer of percussion. It was jazz, the pianist Ahmad Jamal in particular. They both had this way of producing staggered notes that sat just behind the beat. In Pos's case, it gave the music a polyrhythmic sound, as if there were two songs going at once. Dave deployed a plainspoken artfulness, the big brother giving you real talk. He was the type who'd support while keeping you on the path to realizing your full potential. Of course he had acerbic standout rhymes on "Itsoweezee (Hot)" and "Stakes Is High," but he also had tracks like "Oooh.," the lead single from *Mosaic Thump*, where—if nothing else—he just wanted to be treated fairly.

When combined, Pos and Dave emitted a psychedelic essence that was strange yet familiar, with rhymes that were tough to pin down yet no less enthralling. Though you could split one from the other and get the same virtuosity, their music as De La Soul was always exact—an organized coil of tightly woven rhymes and choruses folded into neat lyrical structures. That sent the lyrics one way; running concurrently, or sometimes divergently, were the patchwork beats that held their own without words at all. No De La albums were dominated by one MC. While they'd occasionally cede the floor to each other, they both maintained a strong presence throughout the entirety of the LP, even if the conceptual theme was driven by one or the other. Compare that with Tribe: their albums felt dominated by Q-Tip toward the back end. Same with the Roots: Black Thought and Malik B. would go verse for verse for much of the record, then Thought would rap by himself or with outside guests near the album's conclusion. De La wasn't the only group to put up a united front musically; groups like OutKast and Little Brother went bar for bar on their albums too. But where I could pull more standout moments from their respective MCs, I couldn't do that as much with De La. Pos and Dave's blackout verses were closer in orbit.

Ask around, and scene observers all say the same thing: the members of De La Soul were good dudes who, while they had some shit with them, brought joy to those they liked and always made time for fans who came correct and journalists who left an imprint. Everyone has a similar De La story: if you saw one of them on the street, they were cordial, and they'd remember writers who did pieces on them months after the story ran.

In 2016, I spoke with De La about the twenty-fifth anniversary of *De La Soul Is Dead* and was struck by how chill the guys were. The more music you cover, the more you chat with bigger names, and the more you talk with the person they want you to see. The larger the artist, the stricter the media training and the shorter time allotted to get to the human behind the veneer. I didn't get that sense with De La. They spoke openly about the times they had to defend themselves on tour and the overwhelming fatigue they had in the wake of their initial fame.

There's this belief that good guys finish last because they aren't cold-blooded assholes who only care about money. De La debunked that theory. They wrote the blueprint for how to remain relevant for thirty-plus years by simply doing their jobs well and treating people with kindness and respect. It's a tried-and-true way to succeed in any industry. Though there's nothing wrong with a figurative foot in someone's ass here and there, those occurrences should be rare.

I hark back to the last hook on *Stakes*, on the song "Sunshine":

De La is the crew that you must hear, but please don't rush the
* stage*
'Cause even though them stakes are really high, we're really not
* here to race*
We're just here to move your mind and soul with perpetuated
* ease*

That might as well be the group's mission statement: "We're really not here to race." Long before the twenty-four-hour news cycle and the false sense of hurry, the music industry still had a breakneck pace to it, perhaps rooted in the actuality of fledgling label execs trying to generate cash and notoriety before the rap bubble burst. Even then, De La never rushed; they eschewed trends as a way to build long-term sustainability. Most artists can't sustain themselves long-term by following the wave. De La was the first big group to show the possibility of large-scale middle-class existence—the mini-mansion with the two-acre plot, the grill smoke billowing from the backyard, the luxury SUV in the garage. To some aspiring rap stars, this doesn't sound cool at all, but quiet comfort is a fine-enough life you can find in the Maryland suburbs and the Hollywood Hills. De La showed what slow living could look like, and they reminded me of older dudes in my family who lived abundantly but weren't the first ones at happy hour every Friday. Simple nights at home with glasses of brown liquor or watching baseball games with the kids were more attractive than nights of uncertainty in the streets.

My uncles, grandfathers, and father figures exemplified the perpetuated ease that De La spoke of, long before De La. My grandfather Raymond, in particular, grew up in 1920s South Carolina and was a guy who could build you a house, dish out tough love, crack open a Schlitz, cruise his car through the warm summer night, and be just fine. He liked fishing and sitting on the porch, a cinder-block slab with two chairs and a cooler. Then, as a teenager, I had my best friend's father to help guide me along. To Alphonso, watching boxing, playing a game of *Madden*, and spinning records on his turntable was the best way to relax. He still loves to dance and sing, and might be the first person to get the party started—at least to me, he didn't need to be out there.

De La showed Black men my age that relaxation was attainable and that we could remain relevant even in solitude. Whether or not you're doing something public-facing, you don't always have to be in the mix. It wasn't until recently that I realized this aspect of De La Soul's influence. In my younger days, I always felt like I needed to be doing *something*. Free time should be filled with finding more work or finishing some other work. Yet that whole rise-n-grind mentality isn't so cute when you're thirty and the doctor says you meet the threshold for hypertension. The work doesn't seem so pressing when you're forty and your cholesterol is a tad too high, and you're concerned that the stress of said work could lead to a heart attack. The worry of keeping up also recedes when you start seeing your rap heroes die close to or in their fifties. Dave, MF DOOM, Biz Markie, DMX, Black Rob, Shock G, Ecstasy (of Whodini). I'm not saying they were trying to keep up with anything, but seeing Black men only ten years my senior transition forced me to reevaluate my own moves. Maybe eat that kale salad instead of the hamburger. Go ahead and walk those thirty minutes instead of waiting for the subway. More water, less liquor. De La's dedication to happiness and self-care didn't connect until I started prioritizing it for myself. And that didn't happen until I started doing therapy. Eating healthy and resting don't land when you're in your twenties. There is no perpetuated ease when you can play basketball for several hours Saturday afternoon and go out on a date that night. The ease hits when your bones make noise and the sheer thought of playing ball makes your Achilles' heel twitch. I exist because De La existed. Because of the way they operated and the lessons they taught. I exist because I prioritized the spiritual essence they exuded as I grew into adulthood. Even now as I sometimes struggle to find ease in the 2020s, I'm reminded of the pace at which De La has navigated three decades of prosperity: make the best art possible, and don't worry about being seen. If you move with integrity and create things rooted in sincerity, good attention will come. You won't have to look for it. You can't make people recognize or appreciate your talent; put out good work and move on.

Slowing down also brings the future into view, a fact that arose on *Mosaic Thump* and the AOI series in general. Here, it sounded as if the group members were looking beyond music and envisioning some sort of normalcy. Peace of mind was paramount. Something as simple as Maseo running through the alphabet with his young son Chauncey moves us into "older De La." Not only is it a tender moment between father and son, but it's a reminder of what life is really all about: the genuine relationships that last beyond the albums and tour dates. Same with the opening song "U Can Do (Life)," on which Pos and Dave take stock of how far they've come in their ten years in the spotlight, but with the sarcastic self-deprecation that had become commonplace in their music. "I'm that full-time rapper, the nickname's Llama," Pos said. "Part-time father if you ask my daughters' mommas." The word "life" was working hardest in the title; after a decade of success, failure, and trauma, Pos, Dave, and Maseo sought a reset. The "life" aspect of work-life balance became the most attractive. And they were finally at a place mentally and financially to lean into it. Where others might adopt a serious tone when it comes to parenthood—or, worse, blame their children's mothers for their own shortcomings—Pos was self-aware enough to jab himself, whether or not the sentiment was true. For his part, Dave chose to envision a panacea that he wouldn't see. "I wanna see the world ten times over," he rapped. "Dive off cliffs and land on opportunities unthinkable."

Here, on an album released in 2000, Dave was looking ahead, envisioning a quiet life in some foreign, faraway place. Hearing it today, it feels like a precursor—much like everything De La did—to what the Los Angeles rapper/producer Tyler, the Creator, posited on his 2021 Grammy-winning rap album, *Call Me If You Get Lost*. To him, flying to tropical islands was both a flex and a blessing that he didn't take for granted, an adventure through which he could simply get away from the hustle and bustle of LA. I heard Dave evince a similar tone, even if he breathed a sense of longing and resignation. When Dave spit, you could always hear the sigh in his voice, the hoping for peace that was just beyond his grasp. And where Tyler came off as a self-made man whose idiosyncrasies finally caught on with listeners, Dave rapped as if diving off cliffs was the last thing left to do—if only he could get to that type of tranquility before it was too late.

There were similarities between *Mosaic Thump* and *3 Feet High and Rising*, even though the latter was far superior. Where listeners had to search harder for the fun on *Stakes Is High*, *Mosaic Thump* had this unbridled joy to it, a high-key fuckitness that had been missing from the band's recent work. The beats felt light and airy, the samples buoyant, the rhythms festive. Beats stalled out and stuttered; songs like "My Writes"—a massive posse cut featuring Xzibit and J-Ro and Tash from the West Coast rap crew Tha Alkaholiks—and the electric party anthem "I.C. Y'all," with Busta Rhymes, weren't about anything in particular. It was rapping for the sake of rapping, an approach the group really hadn't taken since earlier in their career. It was refreshing to hear the irreverence of the "ghost weed" skits and the '80s-centered B-boy aesthetic of "Squat!," another posse cut, featuring Ad-Rock and Mike D of Beastie Boys. It was the most feature-heavy album in De La's discography and a victory lap of sorts.

In years past, either among themselves or with their initial producer, Prince Paul, the band tended to keep features relegated to those close to their universe. By including a wider group of voices, De La opened their sound to different avenues and perspectives, giving their later music broader universality.

If there are flash points on the album, they are "Oooh." and "All Good?," featuring the soul singer Chaka Khan. The former was a high-wire call-and-response that quickly became an anthem, thanks mostly to Redman's off-the-wall, all-caps prompts that went beyond De La's comfort zone. But this was a newer, rowdier De La, a fascinating blend of exhilarated calm. For their parts, Pos and Dave kept it chill, throwing subtle shots at Tommy Boy, shiny-suit rappers, and flossing MCs. Redman was a sledgehammer, shouting out "fat chicks" getting their "fuck on tonight." "All Good?" was a not-so-subtle shot at those who abandoned the group once sales dropped and commercial appeal dissipated. Once again, instead of laying the blame elsewhere, Pos pokes fun at himself and the group for saying what we all knew:

We were certified hot, then dropped to lukewarm
Now we back up in the spot, claimin' "never been gone"
Niggas who cut us off wanna reattach us now
Them girls who brushed us off, say they want some numbers to dial

At this stage of De La's career, with their cultural status solidified, the band didn't have anything to lose. Just throw everything against the wall and see what sticks. Though *Mosaic Thump* played like a last-stand, kitchen-sink record with the same jovial spirit of the flower-and-pastel days, the album was just OK, too rife with filler to stand tall on its own. Did it have joints on it? Sure. I still play "Oooh." at an insane volume on headphones and in the car. But *Mosaic Thump* marked the first time I couldn't play a De La album front to back and gather something new from it. I found that I played the album simply because it was De La, and I wanted to support whatever they were doing. While I wanted to cast myself as some music scholar who knew everything there was to know about *real hip-hop*, I was ultimately just a fan who wanted to hear the group drop a great record. But not just great—great in the way I wanted it to be great. Great like the others were great. To my ear, *Mosaic Thump* was the glossiest album of De La's to that point. It was a little too pop-leaning, too buttoned-up and clean. *Mosaic Thump* tried splitting the difference between underground ideals and commercial success, which made the album feel uneven. In an attempt to be everything to disparate groups of people, the product they released didn't have much soul.

By the time *Mosaic Thump* came out, I was a sophomore in college. I wrote stories for the school newspaper and started going to open-mic showcases on campus. Alongside a way-too-packed course load, my best friend and I used to play *NBA Live* and *Madden* on PlayStation, often leaving the room door open so others could walk in, chill, and play a game if they wanted. If I wasn't on the game controller, I was in the back playing CDs way too loudly. One of those CDs was *Mosaic Thump*, because I felt I had to. I was just one voice of millions in the De La congregation, but I still felt protective of them as an admirer. So I'd play the record in full, even though I didn't fully enjoy what I was hearing. I felt I needed to shout out the group because they needed the support. The suitemates who came through didn't mind the music, but I noticed they didn't lean into it either. At least not in the way that I was used to seeing listeners lean into De La. This marked the first time that a De La album was just sort of *there*. Just floating along in the background.

For every jam, there were other songs that didn't quite do anything and just sort of existed because they could. Songs like

"With Me" and "Copa (Cabanga)" didn't embody the De La spirit to which I'd been accustomed. They played like no-frills party records, akin to the style of rap the group had lambasted. While we celebrated others for sampling familiar soul records and looping them into palatable dance tracks, the technique seemed beneath De La's capability and felt a little too easy. Easy is fine, but it's ironic within the context of musicians who never played it safe. And that's how *Mosaic Thump* felt: safe. De La's safe was still better than others' most creative efforts, but De La had never phoned it in. And parts of the album felt phoned in. It also felt like they were playing catch-up, which to me was odd and sad. It felt like maybe these would be De La's last albums, that this was a curtain call. Maybe life beckoned.

The second album of the planned trilogy, *AOI: Bionix*, which was released in late 2001, skewed closer to De La's aura as a narrative-driven LP along the lines of *De La Soul Is Dead*. Of the albums in the AOI series, these tracks resonated longer beyond initial consumption, despite the LP's uneven play as well. While the title track presented a clever side of De La, with Pos making considerable use of double entendres, other songs like "Baby Phat," "Special," and "Pawn Star" were love-and-lust joints that didn't sound natural. In fact, they sounded forced. But the highs were higher on *Bionix*, like on "Held Down," a brilliant gospel-centered song featuring Cee-Lo Green; "Peer Pressure," featuring J Dilla and B-Real from the rap trio Cypress Hill; and "Trying People," a heartfelt ode to staying the course amid a changing national landscape. "Held Down" and "Trying People" were vulnerable, the former a Pos-led solo track about being positive in a world that doesn't always reward such behavior. He also spoke of the proximity between the righteous and the wicked, and how we're all a few steps from darkness, no matter how much we pretend to be above it. The golden child in your neighborhood has the same chemical makeup as the troubled kid. They're from the same place and endured similar challenges; the only difference is one was "diagnosed with a bad case of that proper upbringing" and didn't fall victim to the circumstances of the environment. This part of the song hit hardest for me as a so-called gifted child who was deemed "tailor-made for bigger and better things," as Pos rapped on the track. This existence has given me serious bouts of survivor's remorse and gifted-child syndrome. The feeling of not fitting in never leaves. "And what does it bring?" Pos continued. "I tell you for me, it brought jealousy and back wounds from all the stabbin' / Cats posin' as my fam just to get grabbin' what's mine."

Perhaps on purpose, the best songs on *Bionix* were somber. The album, released December 4, 2001, arrived almost three months after the September 11 terrorist attacks. While the album was finished well before, it landed at a time when listeners couldn't fathom what was next for a nation that hadn't been bludgeoned that brutally. I was still living in Landover. That morning, my mother, who worked for the Department of Justice, called me when the commercial airliner hit the Pentagon, breaking the news to me before the local station did. In an instant, everything felt bleak, cold, dystopian. Dave spoke to this on what might be his manifesto, "Trying People," the album's introspective concluding track. I'd never heard him so openhearted, pensive, and resolute. Listening to it now, though, it's unfortunate to hear the rapper envision a life without kids and bills, before worldly pressures had set in. And when he says, "When I'm gone, make sure the headstone reads, 'He did it for us,'" not only does it hit harder because he's since transitioned, but he's addressing a segment of men who put their loved ones first to the detriment of their own health and well-being. Men of a certain generation were taught by older men to protect and provide for their wives and children at any cost. In turn, they don't prioritize self-care and often feel burned out by the constant churn of dutiful service to others.

I know this because I struggled with this too. Now, I take pride in being the best friend and family member possible. Yet in years past I employed this head-down, get-it-done approach at the peril of my own mental and physical well-being. Though I still take joy in showing up for others, I realized I couldn't do that without showing up for myself first. And that's another lesson learned from certain songs on *Bionix* and from the AOI series in general. Where *Mosaic Thump* resembled the old person in the room trying to recapture their youth, parts of *Bionix* pulled back the curtain on how De La felt about aging. It revealed pronounced battle scars from the wear and tear of growing up in the music business and unpacked the push and pull of loving and resenting the journey. This was De La at the crossroads of their personal and professional lives, feeling thankful but also disappointed that financial circumstances and social status aren't where they'd like them to be.

As was the case with anything De La–related in those days, AOI was driven by frustration and false starts. The band renegotiated its contract before *Bionix*—its sixth album—was released, and with a new deal in place, De La felt better about their future at Tommy Boy, the only label they'd ever known. Despite a new contract and a few extra dollars in their respective pockets, De La didn't feel supported creatively, which cut deep given that they helped make the label relevant. After a decade there, they wanted to leave. The band ultimately got their wish, but not in the way they envisioned.

Shortly after the release of *Bionix*, Tommy Boy Records hit the skids financially and had to scrap the third album, a DJ-centered LP meant to feature Maseo. The label, though it operated independently, had been in a joint venture with Warner Music Group since 1985. The partnership reportedly came to an end after Warner pressed for bigger sales and more acts that could garner mainstream acceptance. Tom

Silverman, under the name Tommy Boy Entertainment, wanted to release the kind of music he did in the early '80s without focusing on numbers. "We're going to return to the foundation that Tommy Boy built its reputation on," Silverman said in 2002. "We'll be investing in what's hot and new in dance/electronic, an area of music that the majors just don't give a shit about. Majors need million-sellers, while we can make a nice profit from records that sell 125,000 copies." Lost in that shuffle was De La. As part of the deal with Warner, they acquired Tommy Boy's catalog and publishing, along with the artists of its roster.

De La was then moved to Elektra Records, which boasted names like Missy Elliott, Busta Rhymes, and Fabolous on its roster. The band seemed excited for a fresh start on a new label. "We feel very happy honestly. Relieved to be on a label that is competing and wants to win," Pos said then. "In the latter years, the heads of Tommy Boy didn't seem to want to win. There were a lot of great people at Tommy Boy who worked really hard, but their hands were tied." The label would have a tough time navigating the new landscape. This wasn't 1988, and listeners weren't clamoring for the latest and greatest Tommy Boy release. In the early 2000s, the type of East Coast hip-hop on which the label was built was a thing of the past. Jay-Z was the game's biggest superstar, and Southern rap made strong inroads. Master P's No Limit Records churned out a steady stream of noted rap albums, and Cash Money Records—powered by the rappers Juvenile, B.G., and Hot Boys—were ushering New Orleans hip-hop into the mainstream. As party songs dominated the airwaves, one would be hard-pressed to hear the type of lyrical complexity from years past on major FM radio. It was there, sure, but only in spurts.

No matter how great De La felt about a potential fresh start, the third AOI album wouldn't come to pass. "We're just going to go back in the studio and concentrate on making a dope De La album," Pos continued. "We may have an *AOI 3* on the Internet for hardcore De La fans, but a DJ-centered album isn't really going to fly with Sylvia Rhone [the head of Elektra]." As it was, De La went back to the lab revitalized and tried to channel that energy into the music. But there was a new battle on the way, one that would define their narrative for the next twenty years: digital streaming.

9

A CATALOG ALMOST LOST TO TIME

N 1999, SHAWN FANNING AND SEAN PARKER CREATED A SOFTWARE program called Napster, a peer-to-peer service on which users could share MP3s for free. Naturally, artists and industry types were squeamish; it was a move that could upend the music business as they knew it. Plus no one really knew what to make of it. Four months into Napster's existence, the Recording Industry Association of America (RIAA) filed a lawsuit against Napster, as did the producer Dr. Dre and the metal band Metallica, after unfinished tracks were uploaded on the site in 2000. The advent of Napster led to other pirate sites—Audiogalaxy, LimeWire, Kazaa, Soulseek, and others—which led to more copyright infringement lawsuits and takedown notices. Though these sites didn't last long, the gauntlet had been thrown: at its peak, Napster averaged eighty million listeners per month. Listeners now expected their music at no cost, and piracy was here to stay.

Music executives contended that online piracy led to declining revenues. Between 1999 and 2008, according to the economist Joel Waldfogel, annual US revenue from physical recorded music products fell from $12.8 billion to $5.5 billion. With digital sales included, Waldfogel reported, US revenue was a third below its 1999 numbers. Worldwide, revenue from physical recorded music dropped to $25 billion in 2007 from $37 billion in 1999. Though these numbers seem relatively high—$25 billion is still a lot of money—the drop-off was significant. At the heart of the issue were the following questions: Just how much does illegal downloading affect the music industry's bottom line? If listeners could download their favorite songs and alternative ones for free, would they still buy physical music? The results were, and still are, tough to pin down: while the RIAA claimed the US economy loses more than $12 billion in total output as a result of music piracy, other reports have been inconclusive. Some analysts attributed the decline to the actual drop in CDs being released since 1999. In the 2010s, when platforms like Spotify and Deezer were instituted as legal music streaming platforms, artists complained of the money they'd get per stream.

De La didn't even get the chance to complain. Their music wasn't streamable. The group was still operating under a record deal that didn't take digital sales into account. Because they sampled so heavily, and some of those clips had to be recleared for newer digital models, record execs got uneasy when dealing with the band. It was just too much to clear, so they'd rather not deal with De La's music at all. "Our contracts on those early albums said specifically 'vinyl and cassette,'" Pos once explained. "The wording wasn't vague enough to lend itself to [new] music technology. So once the whole age of digital music came into play, new deals needed to be cut for those entire albums."

This started a slow trickle for the group. With the AOI series still fresh and a follow-up album, *The Grind Date*, on the horizon, it was easy to forget that the earlier music wasn't streaming. That, coupled with the sheer volume of songs and albums that flooded the marketplace, pushed *3 Feet High*, . . . *Is Dead, Buhloone*, and *Stakes* further into the rear view. Undaunted, the band kept touring the old material, not really pressed about the music not being around, since the group was still putting out music. In those days, the Internet was still a burgeoning marketplace that few knew what to do with. I was working as a reporter at a local newspaper in Maryland at the time, and our CEO would sometimes hold company-wide meetings to dole out good news and also discuss "this thing called the Internet." It was a weird dialogue, given that the Web was already eating into our ad revenue. Yet the Web was still this amorphous thing that threatened the livelihood not only of the newspaper but of all industries offering paid services to consumers. The Web provided immediacy.

De La released *The Grind Date* in 2004 through the indie Sanctuary Urban imprint, as the Tommy Boy and Warner merger was in limbo, scrapping the third AOI album altogether for a completely new work. With the band's future in jeopardy, they returned with a lean offering that cut out the filler of their previous albums for a tighter, refined sound dedicated to the upcoming crop of underground producers and MCs. In that way, *The Grind Date* felt like an overt dedication to their truest creative sensibilities. It was also a veteran's album, the equivalent of a grizzled athlete who's been in the league and doesn't trip off the new hotshot rookie being propped up by the media. This was De La's chance to show love to the younger guys who inspired them—producers like Madlib, 9th Wonder, Supa Dave West, and Jake One. I consumed this album as a grown man, no longer in school. I'd been so used to listening to De La as an extracurricular practice alongside the formal education I was receiving when their music was released. So it was something else to play the group's music as an adult with bills, a job, and a car. Without noticing, I'd grown up with De La Soul.

For the first time in a while, De La was able to amass a full project that didn't feel clogged with unnecessary fodder that disrupted the flow of the music. In turn, the LP held some of the most rewindable work in its discography, especially the concluding track, "Rock Co.Kane Flow," a stuttering epic featuring an invigorated Pos and Dave rapping alongside MF DOOM. Equally present and forward-looking, other songs like "The Future" and "Verbal Clap" were simultaneously wistful and combative, joints that reminded fans of the sweet, edgy energy of the band's golden era. But the album landed at what might be the lowest point ever for rap music and hip-hop culture as a whole. There wasn't a lot of good hip-hop being released, at least not the kind I'd want to play.

Though there was a young Chicago producer and rapper named Kanye West who brought energy to the game as a hybrid of underground and mainstream, the seeds of the shiny-suit era bore fruit beyond what the OGs could handle. Save for a few albums—Madlib and MF DOOM, in particular, released the collaborative *Madvillainy* to enormous acclaim—2004 was littered with disappointing projects from established acts who seemed tapped out on music altogether. It was either too easy, too celebratory, or just flat-out underwhelming. Rap was a little too melodic for my taste, not funky or impactful enough. Even another favorite rap group of mine, the Roots, released an album called *The Tipping Point* that felt too caught up in pop culture gloss for me to get into it. I twisted myself in knots trying to like that album. And I was conflicted because I wanted the Roots to get their money, but I hoped they'd have a better LP to do it with. All the emphasis on bottle service reopened the door for De La to slide in undetected. *The Grind Date* wasn't one of their best albums, but at least it showed that the guys still cared, even at a time when the public at large wasn't checking for new De La projects.

The band's releasing new music and touring distracted from the fact that they didn't have a digital presence. In subsequent years, with the band on hiatus and streaming as the primary source of music consumption, the amount of money and attention being missed out on became too much to ignore—especially since everyone else's catalog (or so it seemed) was readily available. Slowly, listeners like me started wondering why we couldn't hit up iTunes and play "Patti Dooke" on the move. Not that we didn't have the CDs or vinyl, but being able to play it from an MP3 player in your pocket seemed easier than playing it on a Discman where slight bumps would cause the plastic to skip.

For a band that was always so deep into the future, it seemed criminal not to have De La be a part of the tech revolution. The band's absence from streaming encouraged an underground network of, well, bootlegging: if you didn't have any of the old records, you'd ask somebody who might, and they'd slide you a copy privately. This wasn't a new practice, of course: we'd been dubbing cassettes and passing them to each other since the '80s, but the fact that we had to do that with De La didn't feel right. They deserved to earn a living like their contemporaries; trading their music took away from their bottom line.

Yet De La's music lent itself to this type of existence. As much as their absence from streaming held them back, it also furthered their legend. That their music wasn't available fed into a ravenous obsession with the group. The hunt for old De La emulated the crate-digging one would do for old music to create new beats. It encouraged demand, which encouraged the trading of their music privately. I also thought, even before the 2010s, that maybe the band didn't mind. The guys always struck me as artists first, not so tethered to the business aspects of the industry. I can also acknowledge that maybe it's an irrational thought within the context of anyone doing something they love and it being stolen. But perhaps they'd rather people just have the music and sort out the business later. These are the thoughts of a twentysomething Marcus who simply wanted *De La Soul Is Dead* on his iPod.

They proved this theory right in 2014 when, frustrated with the lack of movement by Warner Bros. (which owned the catalog), they released their golden-era records on the Internet for free for a day. The response was so overwhelming that it crashed the servers. The move, Dave said, was partially meant to celebrate the twenty-fifth anniversary of *3 Feet High and Rising* by getting the album out of limbo and to the people who deserved it most: the fans. "We thought that would be the best gift after twenty-five years," he continued. "And sort of a statement to say that we're frustrated. You know, let's put all our catalog for twenty-five hours on the Internet and let people just take it." Their priority, then and always, was to get their work out there. Just let it live. The rest will shake out somehow. This move, like others throughout their career, was a calculated risk, a bold leap from a group that always operated fearlessly. Doing this helped De La amass a dedicated legion of supporters who, in turn, supported their music in spaces far beyond hip-hop. These same supporters, some of them in high places, would prove vital to De La's livelihood in the coming years.

It became tougher for the band to find traction within the industry machine. The employees who once supported the music either got promoted or left for other work and were replaced with staffers who weren't around during De La's heyday. As a result, there wasn't enough verve from the label side to fight for the group's legacy. The industry is full of folks with short memories, which fuels the constant need for the next trend or hot rapper. This also speaks to a common annoyance with the business model as a whole: it can be run by people who don't know good music and can't spot what is intriguing. Instead of trying to find artists who dare to be different, they prioritize acts making the same music as someone else. The goal is to generate revenue, so if said artist can bolster the company's bottom line, that's what matters.

This wasn't a new practice, mind you: after the release of Miles Davis's *Bitches Brew* and its huge commercial success, countless jazz musicians started blending the genre with facets of funk and rock in hopes of emulating the groundbreaking LP. Having worked in the industry as hip-hop director at a vinyl subscription service, I'd sometimes have to deal with employees at some major labels who, quite frankly, seemed fine doing the bare minimum. Given the economy at the time, it was as if they were doing enough not to get fired. I never dealt with De La's label during my time at the service, but ultimately De La suffered because of this kind of prevalent thinking throughout the business. They were never the type of turnkey band that didn't need some type of support from someone in-house who understood their status as musical aliens. They still needed some sort of primer or explanation, and even then, that might not encapsulate the breadth of what they were doing on those records. And, sadly, there didn't seem to be many around who even had the capacity to explain. There weren't crowds like in years past who *got it*. After years of not having their music online, the band just sorta got used to it and resigned themselves to making money touring and featuring on other artists' projects. The urge to get their music to the masses was still there, but without many people in their corner, hope diminished. It was as if the industry had forgotten about De La.

BY 2009, I WAS A FULL-ON ADULT WITH A LONGTIME ON-AGAIN, OFF-AGAIN girlfriend who I'd gotten back together with that year. I was also tired of covering education for that local newspaper. It was a cool-enough gig, one that I appreciated and took seriously. But three years into it, I could predict what was going to happen at the school board meetings and council committees. I deepened my connection with local music as a way to sharpen my skills as a critic and journalist. It was the blog era, so I launched a culture site with news, features, and reviews called *DMV Spectrum* (the acronym stood for DC, Maryland, and Virginia). As I saw it, my faves were all either done or between albums, so there wasn't much reason for me to pay attention to mainstream rap at all. Q-Tip had delved into making psychedelic jazz albums under the name Kamaal the Abstract, and there was this new rapper named Drake who I thought was cool, but I could tell early on that he wasn't for me. I was listening to a little bit of everything—Maxwell, Sa-Ra Creative Partners, Flying Lotus—but there was no central theme to what I consumed. One day it could be an old Janet Jackson song, the next it could be a new indie rapper from Virginia. I turned my attention to the DC area, to rappers like yU, groups like Gods'Illa, and virtuosos like Kokayi. I went to open mics to learn everything I could about all the micro-scenes within the larger local one, and that required my full attention. Every weekend, and occasionally during weekday evenings, I'd drive to showcases all over the region to see what was weird and intriguing. The routine helped me build lasting connections with regional artists, some of whom I consider family.

One day, I was browsing through the new releases section on iTunes when I noticed something I hadn't seen in five years: a new album by De La Soul. I don't remember any marketing for it at all. It was just . . . there. The album was called *Are You In?: Nike+ Original Run* and was a mixtape made in collaboration with Nike. Naturally, I checked it out and was taken right away by a voice I heard at the onset: Raheem DeVaughn, a noted DC singer who was something of a star in the region. Hearing Raheem rock with De La bridged two distinct worlds for me—one rooted in the past and tapping into an upbringing listening to my favorite group, the other a new horizon that I was just now discovering in my hometown. Largely produced and mixed by the DJ duo Flosstradamus, it was full of cavernous funk and breakbeats and meant to be consumed in one continuous playback. It was also the most inspired De La had sounded in years. It didn't feel as if the group was looking to make a statement or run down commercial rap tropes. Rather, the guys just rapped. About anything, about nothing, about how much better they were than you, about getting up and seizing the day. It was refreshing to hear. Though it was meant to soundtrack a forty-five-minute run (it was sponsored by Nike after all), it was a surprisingly good reminder of what De La could do when fun was the foremost objective.

But even at their happiest, the guys couldn't resist lamenting their shortcomings in the business. "Some say the game's rigged, 'cause the man didn't give us manuals to the game to make it big," Pos decried on "Big Mouf," one of a few album standouts. In an effective yet somewhat passive-aggressive way, the band showed they still mistrusted Tommy Boy Records while gathering more support for their plight. Their lyrics placed the blame solely at the label's feet and garnered sympathy from staunch fans and passersby who identified with the issue. Who among us hasn't dealt with supervisors we didn't like, but we still had to work with the person and within the system? Livelihood and whatnot. At a certain point, you just have to suck it up and deal with the foolishness and try to find some form of joy within the distress, or beyond the workplace altogether.

De La's anguish was everyone's anguish; their bitterness resonated with much of the workforce. It also landed with me. By that point, I had grown tired of the day-to-day grind of driving thirty-plus miles to a newsroom run by executives whose vision I no longer believed in. My closest colleagues were either leaving or checked out, and it became tougher to work a beat that no longer excited me. That's a small example compared to De La's strife, but the situation armed me with an understanding of having to maneuver in corporate confines that don't fit. I was never just one thing, and neither was the band. Despite the industry—be it small newspapers or music—it's easy to feel like you don't have options, even if that's not the case at all.

Letting listeners into what was really happening wasn't foreign to De La, but they also ran the risk of wearing out fans who wanted to rock with the group but didn't always want to hear Tommy Boy–related banter. I'm not here to tell De La what they should've done, of course, but I often wondered what the resolution could be for this seemingly dire situation with no end in sight. Could De La force Tommy Boy and Warner's hand and secure a rightful resolution? I sure hoped so. My naive brain wanted to believe that the game would look out for a group that brought so much joy and creativity to pop culture. But it wasn't until I got older that I learned the following: that's not how things work. Even if the band had allies working on their behalf, it would take years to pore over old contracts and cut through the red tape binding all of them. So, without immediate recourse and with no real way out of their situation, De La just waited. And waited . . . and waited.

In the group's absence, the excitement around streaming only increased, thanks to the launch of Spotify, making it tougher for quality acts to break through. Slowly, the metrics surrounding what constituted a successful release switched from how many records were sold to how many streams the record received. This allowed the big names to stay big: the dopamine of seeing your project rack up millions of streams rivaled the feeling of watching CDs and vinyl fly out the door.

But here's a phenomenon I've noticed in the many years I've been covering music: The underground carries the torch for the rest of mainstream music. Sure, musicians like Taylor Swift and Beyoncé will always set trends, but I've seen a current of esoteric, left-of-center acts become standard-bearers for what listeners consumed in the 2010s and 2020s. I'm not saying that listeners have ignored major artists, or that they should. The classics are the classics for a reason, and records like *Renaissance* (Bey's critically acclaimed 2022 album) deserve all the love being bestowed upon them. Yet there's a growing number of people who'd rather hear the undermarketed dope shit emerging from musicians like the vocalist Nick Hakim, the violinist/producer/singer Sudan Archives, and the alt-soul of the singer Liv.e. These are the ones who maybe don't have the same press, but the music—though challenging—always rewards listeners looking for something fresh and intriguing. I'm often asked what I'm listening to. There's little to no interest when I respond with a mainstream artist. It's when I go up about artists like Joel Ross, Brandee Younger, Melanie Charles, or Kadhja Bonet that the smartphones come out and the notes apps open. Listeners want to discover something new, not be subjected to something they can get from an algorithm. It's also why legacy artists like Alice Coltrane can enjoy a renaissance now. Though she was signed to major labels in her day, the music she put forth—astral, string-laden cosmic jazz—stood as a heartfelt tribute to what we cannot see and other stimuli we underappreciate: that thing just beyond comprehension that you can feel but can't fathom.

The tide turned during the streaming era, a time in which anyone with a smartphone and a Wi-Fi connection could upload their music to Myspace and SoundCloud and have listeners. This gave rise to a community of lo-fi beatmakers and bedroom pop artists crafting songs from their private living spaces. But where groups like De La and other OGs used their demo recordings as a proving ground for what could and couldn't work in the studio, the new kids were uploading music with a new kind of intimacy. They let the mistakes and shoddy mixing stay in there. At its core, underground music felt closer to everyday people who think about what to eat for dinner and how to keep their kids engaged during the summer months. For those of us not swimming in gold coins, we like to feel a sense of connection to the music we consume. At least I do, anyway.

With the metrics surrounding what constituted a successful release shifting, the world was coming back around to what De La represented all those years ago, even if the band—by arbitrary industry rules—was too old to be considered viable. Still, what I was hearing from the likes of Knxwledge and Mndsgn (pronounced Mind Design) resembled what I'd heard on "Plug Tunin'" all those years ago. The dust in the speakers. The woozy, off-kilter drum programming. I can't say definitively that they were overtly influenced by Prince Paul and De La, but the connections were too strong to deny. The DNA of what Paul, Pos, Dave, and Maseo did all the way back in 1987 after school in a nondescript single-family home in Amityville, just messing around, shaking creative tables, was still bearing fruit in the 2010s and 2020s. De La was able to sustain themselves amid a myriad of trends in both hip-hop and pop culture overall, and—as styles tend to do over the course of generations—the barometer shifted back toward putting out weird and adventurous art that offended traditional sensibilities.

Trends fade, and despite the hubbub surrounding real versus fake hip-hop, underground versus mainstream, gold and platinum versus flopping and going wood, De La was rap's best example of what can happen when you ignore what's expected. Was it tough? Of course it was. No one truly appreciates the trendsetter when they're setting the trends, and fewer people even tried to figure out De La as the calendar turned. There's something noble about building a career organically, by challenging your listeners at every turn, by simply doing something different that scrambles the heads of stuffy critics projecting their preferences onto your art. Yet risk-taking is lonely. Along the road less traveled lies occasional self-doubt and worry about what to do next and how to get people to understand your perspective.

As De La's mystique has grown, younger listeners took to illegal uploads on YouTube and started doing their own digging into the group. Or they'd buy original physical copies of its pre-2004 catalog for hundreds of dollars on Discogs or eBay. That kept the band's music alive and its name at the forefront. In 2010, the Library of Congress added *3 Feet High and Rising* to its National Recording Registry based on its "cultural significance and general excellence." Still, as Pos told *Rolling Stone* in 2014, "We've been blessed to be in the Library of Congress, but we can't even have our music on iTunes. It's been a trying journey."

EVERY SO OFTEN, DE LA WOULD REEMERGE WITH A STAND-ALONE SINGLE OR guest feature to let fans know they were still around. In 2013, the band released "Get Away (feat. the Spirit of Wu-Tang)" as yet another kiss-off to rappers trifling with the essence of hip-hop, which was to innovate and evolve. "Everything is redundant," Maseo said then. "Everything sounds the same. No real lyrical content. Everybody's just doing business, not really creating." Sampling a skit from the Wu's 1997 album *Wu-Tang Forever*, "Get Away" was the first single the group released during the convergence of iTunes and social media, where fans could take to sites like Facebook and Twitter and chat about the song in real time. So it only made sense that De La would come back with a track like this, in an era like this, as a way to reintroduce older listeners to and school newer ones on the band's iconoclastic perspective. A tough-minded song with thumping drums and sweeping keys, it was one of the harder tracks in the band's late-career discography, but their persistent dismissal of other MCs had worn thin to me.

On the one hand, I totally got it, and I agreed: Mainstream rap had gotten same-y, but at what point do you start crying wolf? How can you chastise your peers for not innovating and challenging creatively when you've been talking about the same thing for years? That's where I found myself at that time, my attention split between covering local rap and subgenres like punk, psychedelic rock, and alternative soul. It was also my first year married, and I needed to settle into some sort of job or make music journalism a thing that could pay some bills and buy groceries. "Two checks are better than one," as my grandfather-in-law said at the wedding reception. With so much going on personally and professionally, and because the immediacy of social media made it tough to actually enjoy a song for a long period, "Get Away" was a dope joint that just sorta slid past me. I could appreciate the track, but eh, let's talk about this second Mac Miller album and Black Milk's *No Poison No Paradise*. And have you heard this Chance the Rapper kid and his mixtape *Acid Rap*? Though the De La single didn't do much to command my attention beyond a few plays, it signaled a comeback. This was the sound that best suited them at this moment of the band's career, and I hoped they would stay with it.

But it also felt weird not to be as infatuated with De La. I still followed the band, but from an aerial perch that took the band's legacy into account. In writing about multihyphenates like Open Mike Eagle, Jean Grae, and Phonte, I was writing about the band's tree and the fruit they bore. What I discovered was that there were legions of supporters just like me ready to help.

In 2015, the group announced it would use Kickstarter, a global crowdfunding platform, to raise money for the recording of a new album. They set a goal of $110,000, with a tiered system of perks depending on how much supporters donated to the cause. Donations of five dollars came with an email of appreciation; pledges of five thousand dollars or more meant you'd join De La for a soundcheck, have dinner with the band, hang out backstage for one of their gigs, be introduced onstage as a special guest, and have VIP access to ten De La shows whenever, wherever. The campaign launch was met with immediate excitement and support from famous fans like Questlove and Chris Rock, as well as everyday people who had a little bit of money to spare for hip-hop's good guys. Still, as much as we reveled in being there for them, they shouldn't have been in this position in the first place. I'm not blaming De La when I say that; it's more an indictment of the machine.

A group like De La should always have the financial backing needed to make the album they want. Just back up the Brink's truck, or give them a blank check, and get out of the way. But for De La to have to do what was essentially busking for change was beneath their stature as legends. Or so I thought; apologies for projecting. De La never hopped up on such pride, though I'm sure I'm not the only one who felt that way. Regardless, it was weird seeing De La giving themselves away on Kickstarter, pawning off their artifacts in order to do what they loved. Perhaps there was another perspective: these same artifacts—the platinum plaques and other industry memorabilia—came with bad memories that they'd rather leave behind. Sometimes it's easier to chuck everything and move forward, and that's what De La was looking to do here. They needed a reset. The band raised $110,000 in nine hours, and a whopping $600,874 in one month—the second-highest amount ever raised on the platform.

Yet the money came with expectations from fans; the album had to be dope. It's bad enough when fans feel they can dictate an artist's movements without financial incentive; it's another when said fans contributed money to the record and it is not what they expected. Yet De La preferred it that way, as they said in 2015. "There were definitely labels interested in De La Soul," Pos told the *New York Times* then. Being beholden to fans alone meant "there's no one in the way, and no one to blame." As a way to circumvent the sample police, who had dogged the band for much of its career, De La spent the better part of three years recording with a live band, with the intention of sampling their music and culling a soundtrack from that.

In essence, De La was sampling itself, which meant no obscure clips to clear and no legal hassles if the sampled artist wanted to chirp about not getting paid. With this vast collective, De La captured more than two hundred hours of raw, improvised arrangements at Vox, the oldest independent recording studio in Los Angeles.

Recording the music there gave the sound its warm texture, the feeling that it was recorded sometime in the 1960s or '70s, thus giving the band's forthcoming album a wistful aura. "In our world," De La wrote on their Kickstarter page, "what we've created is freedom, freedom to make the art you believe in without having to compromise your vision." The band, which had been indie since 2004, needed funds to record, mix, master, and market a product that wasn't chasing hit singles, chart-topping success, or Grammy Awards. The goal was simply to make a good album that resonated beyond mainstream parameters long after its release.

It would also be the band's most ambitious album, which was saying a lot. A mix of rap, jazz, funk, rock, and country, it was slated to be a grand effort that fully represented its artistic sensibilities. Titled *and the Anonymous Nobody...*, it was a communal effort meant to decenter De La as its main focal point and put the emphasis on the "we" and not the "i" that can often permeate the music industry. As they saw it, selfishness had eroded trust and pushed good people out of the business. The jam sessions and robust features list—an all-star rotation that included the singers Usher and Jill Scott and the rappers Snoop Dogg and 2 Chainz—were made to feel like a compilation project, with artists moving in and out of the LP like performers at an open mic. The band wasn't looking for singles or radio airplay, and they weren't being stressed by a label to produce a hit. It led to an ambitious offering that didn't land with the impact that I'd hoped.

That's where I felt conflicted, and where I agreed with artists who'd rather not ask fans for financial help when it comes to art. The problem, I thought, was that the album didn't know what it wanted to be. And in the process of making a project with everything, it felt unfocused and too vast.

It also put me in a weird space because, for the first time, there was a De La album that I didn't like. Where songs like "Property of Spitkicker.com," featuring the popular Buffalo-bred rapper Roc Marciano, and "Memory of . . . (Us)," featuring the singer Estelle, showed flashes of the old De La—the former a skittering beat with metallic synths, the latter a symphonic soul track with lovelorn rhymes about romance gone by—the rest was scattered and unsettled, as if they were trying to please everyone who contributed to the campaign.

That's how I felt as a fan. I wanted to hear De La do the raw shit, not spit rhymes over blaring guitars. I wanted to like it more, because of who they were and what they meant to me and others like me. I did what any fan does: compare it to previous work, hoping foolishly that somehow they'd be able to reignite the fire of albums gone by.

But it wasn't until I relistened that I understood what was happening: since the band got its record deal, they'd had to perform under some sort of parameter, even if it meant just giving the record label a single to promote. For the better part of two decades, the group had to fight to simply keep its smile intact, to create the art they wanted without some nonmusician telling them what they wanted to hear on it.

Without oversight, De La replicated the approach of *De La Soul Is Dead* and *Buhloone Mindstate*, even if their structures felt somewhat controlled, compared with the uninhibited robustness of *3 Feet High and Rising*. The album was met with mixed reviews. Where *SPIN* awarded it an eight out of ten and said that "their creativity has only sharpened," *Pitchfork* gave it a 6.4 and called it "kind of a downer" but acknowledged the band's observational prowess. And where *Clash* called it "an impressive new installment," *Rolling Stone* was less complimentary. *"And the Anonymous Nobody* sometimes risks losing Posdnuos, Dave and Maseo in their own record," wrote the critic Alan Light. "Tracks like the loopy 'Snoopies' (with David Byrne) and old-school throwdown 'Whoodeeni' (with 2 Chainz) are glorious bug-outs, but the urban cautionary tale 'Greyhounds' (echoing Stevie Wonder's 'Living for the City,' with Usher on the hook) is a reminder that De La are often more powerful when they're less goofy—and that their greatest strength has always been not caring what hip-hop is supposed to sound like."

As a kid discovering De La Soul, I didn't have the language to explain what it was I was hearing and why it connected so deeply. Then, as I got older, I found that I still didn't have the capacity to describe how the music molded me, and that was OK. In an industry so hopped up on academic, overwrought explanations of why music is good and what we think the art is saying, it's OK to love music for what it is and not have fifty-dollar words to explain its essence. Sometimes it's fine to sit with something and not have to adhere to some arbitrary timeline, as if the music will somehow dissolve if it isn't assessed within a week of its release date.

As the world gets quicker and attention spans dissipate, De La makes you lean in slowly, to spend time with the music. You'll need time to try to catch all the bars and storytelling anyway. Hell, even three decades into their existence, I still have chats with friends who are just now picking up on some of the rhymes they spat way back when. That is the surest attribute of great music and the ultimate compliment to De La Soul—a band that was, is, and will always be ahead of time, and yet somehow on time.

It's important to acknowledge De La—despite all the superlatives—as just a fun group that created festive, thought-provoking rap. It didn't always need to be overanalyzed or checked off as part of a larger conversation about Black pride. The pride was felt in everything they did. De La Soul was a band that defied comprehension and sound, a band with palpable textures and flaws, a band that I told others about and blasted through my mom's Dodge Dynasty speakers when I first learned to drive.

De La Soul was real-life music for little moments like this, for times we forget and don't appreciate until other memories fade. Did they make the best music all the time? No. I don't think they'd say they did. And was *and the Anonymous Nobody . . .* their best work? Not even close. But honestly, it didn't matter to fans like me who simply wanted them around. As a critic, I wanted to jump in with some suit-n-tie assessment of what the music was doing. But as a fan, I didn't care. Being a journalist and creative writer meant putting myself in the shoes of fans I used to ignore. As a concert reviewer for the *Washington Post*, I used to see people jumping up and down about the artist onstage, blind to the idea that maybe the show wasn't great. I had to look past those folks and just study the gig. The fans were going to scream no matter what. But the *Anonymous Nobody* campaign taught me not to be so stuffy and cynical, even when cynicism permeated their art. Simply enjoy what was happening, and hopefully there's something you can take away from it. That's the most any of us can do as creators and public-facing people pouring our hearts into whatever we make for mass consumption.

And even though I didn't like *Nobody*, others thought differently. It debuted at No. 12 on the Billboard 200 and was the first De La to debut No. 1 on Billboard's Top Rap Albums—a feat that not even *3 Feet High* achieved. It was reportedly streamed two million times in its first week and was nominated for the Grammy for Best Rap Album. De La had reentered a fray as OGs in a field dominated by the likes of Kendrick and Drake. The year 2016, in particular, saw the release of several good albums and others that are considered classics: Solange's *A Seat at the Table*, Frank Ocean's *Blonde*, Beyoncé's *Lemonade*, and Rihanna's *Anti*. Even then, De La garnered headlines. New fans could wonder what it must've been like in 1989, while older fans could revisit those good feelings once more. Though the band always had a weird relationship with numbers and stats, the fact that their new album was played that many times in a short period showed there was an audience for De La. There's a thin line between humility and self-deprecation, and as much as De La wanted to act like they were forgotten by time, the people proved over and over that such thinking was misguided.

Even some of the funding they secured came from beyond De La's expected purview. "There was a reaction from the Kickstarter community, who just are all about being behind or pushing a project that sounds like a great idea," Dave once said. "There was a big part of that community that came and supported us. They might not have been the biggest De La Soul fans, but they understood what we were trying to accomplish and got on board with us." As *Nobody* proved, there were hordes of people and hundreds of thousands of dollars in financial support just waiting to be tapped into. If that album amassed that much attention on streaming platforms, the golden-era albums might break the damn Internet. Sadly, though, it would take a few years for us to get this question answered. False starts and dishonest business kept De La on the shelf for another few years—with incredibly sad occurrences along the way.

THE DOVE FLIES

I SHOULD'VE KNOWN IT WAS TOO GOOD TO BE TRUE. WELL, ACTUALLY, I DID; I was skeptical but held out hope regardless. It was around 2017 when I got word that Tommy Boy had supposedly reacquired the full rights to its catalog and would upload much of it to streaming. I asked a Tommy Boy representative the question that any De La fan would ask:

> *Does that mean that the band's catalog is in the clear, the samples are all signed off, and it'll be uploaded too?*
> We're working on it.

So began a cycle of check-ins and awkward silence that would last roughly six years. A year later, though, the label offered up a reissue of *Buhloone Mindstate*, perhaps signaling the pending arrival of the other records as well. Naturally, I was hyped. "This is not a drill!," or something to that effect, was what I typed to my Twitter followers. Some OG music industry heads whom I respect responded with rightful skepticism. "For real?" went the sentiment; I could almost see the raised eyebrows through my smudgy smartphone screen. But I was willfully ignorant; as far as I knew, the De La catalog was *back*, and I wanted all the vinyl—beginning with the *Buhloone Mindstate* wax that was suddenly available for purchase. Come to find out the vinyl was reissued to capitalize on the record's twenty-fifth anniversary.

"Catalog is not on Bandcamp," label president Rosie Lopez told *HipHopDX* in an email. "We pressed *Buhloone Mindstate* on color vinyl for an exclusive (25th anniversary) Vinyl Me Please release earlier this year and did a small run on black vinyl. Just 300 are available on Bandcamp. 500 copies will find their way into retail stores in November. . . . We are in the process of preserving all analog tapes for all of the albums and plan to remaster and release on vinyl using 24-bit audio next year." Yet "next year" would never come; by 2019, the fight between De La and Tommy Boy reached its worst point.

In February of that year, Tommy Boy announced it would upload De La's full catalog to streaming services, ending thirty years of wrangling over contracts and morale. Details have remained sketchy. As soon as the intention was announced, De La retorted with their own update, using their social media platform to encourage fans not to stream the music when it was uploaded. The deal was a 70–30 split in favor of the label and included a $2 million debt that the band supposedly owed going back to when they first signed in 1988. Not only that, two-thirds of the band's 30 percent would go toward the balance of this debt, rendering De La with only 10 percent of the profit—a fraction of what they deserved.

"Dear Fans," the group wrote on Instagram, "just got off the phone with Tommy Boy Records . . . negotiations (or lack thereof) to release our catalog on all streaming platforms. Uh oh." Calling it an "ugly greedy nightmare," De La kept updating their fans on the negotiations with Tommy Boy—much to the label's chagrin—as a way to keep public pressure on them. At this point in their career, after years of stalled-out negotiations and vitriolic disdain, it seemed social media was the last place they had left to turn, and if they got equally famous people to sympathize with their plight, the label would be forced to do right by them. Finally, De La wasn't laying low and staying out of the way; in their most desperate hour, they were cashing in on the love they'd accrued over the past three decades to see how far they could go.

The full-court press didn't cease. After the band spoke with the label about samples that still weren't cleared for release, the label reportedly wanted to proceed with plans to upload the catalog and deal with lawsuits later. "Really????" the band posted on IG. "That's just not smart business. We don't want to be sued." Moreover, one would assume that the label wouldn't want to endure that again, given its history dealing with lawsuits caused by sample issues. Sure enough, the support started pouring in. First, Tidal—the Norwegian American streaming service affiliated with Jay-Z—said in support of De La that they wouldn't have the band's catalog on the site until the issues were resolved. Then their peers—Nas, Pete Rock, Questlove—once again. The momentum for De La grew with each post, each interview, each write-up. Tommy Boy wanted to negotiate a new deal, but only if the band signed a confidentiality agreement, thus ending the public campaign for the rights to their music. "Feels like they want to silence us to ensure that we cannot share this story with you, while they continue to short change our legacy at the negotiating table," De La wrote at the time.

It did seem odd that the label allegedly would want to upload uncleared samples and perhaps just hope that the suits never arrived. It seems like common sense to get everything squared away so you won't have to worry about it. I can't say what the label's intentions were—they haven't said anything about it publicly, and they didn't respond to requests for comment for this book—but it did feel like they were trying to cash in on the band's music. It's not until you wade through the industry that you realize how common that is. I've heard countless stories of labels signing musicians to perpetuity deals (meaning the label retains the rights to their music forever) and profiting from the musicians' hit records for years and years. The money made from streaming can be significant for these labels; the artist only gets pennies on the dollar. It's a numbers game for these companies: the more music you have up for streaming, the more money you could potentially make. And I've heard from industry insiders over the years that the higher-ups may not even know about the album in question. They don't know how it was created, and they can't speak to its creative intent or critical impact long-term.

Meanwhile, the creator lives and dies for their art. I don't say that hyperbolically. I know and have spoken with several musicians whose anxieties have grown, or whose physical and mental health has faltered, simply because their work means everything to them, and in a capitalist economy that requires them to move mountains to stay afloat, said person has to keep creating just to make ends meet.

It's a fine line that anyone with a dream and a little talent has to cross. The rise-n-grind mentality only leads to hospital visits, a pile of medical bills, and overdue rent, and there's no guarantee that the public will appreciate what you're trying to convey. De La was blessed enough to have felt the love they rightfully deserved, but for other lesser-known and esoteric musicians, the gratitude may arrive when it's too late, when they're either too old or deceased. I've never understood why this is normalized, why we can't show love or, at the very least, respect to those who inspire us publicly. Why does everyone have to be cool? What do you lose by showing emotion and giving someone else their due? It doesn't make you soft or any of that other toxically masculine shit. We should all be here to pay it forward and build sustainable relationships.

Why can't major labels do this? I'm not saying that all execs engage in such behavior, but the music industry is what it is, and we've normalized 70–30 splits and 90–10 deals as the way things are. Because there's little to no pushback and no grand effort to empower musicians, they keep on keepin' on, taking shoddy deals for a quick buck without thinking about the future. For the most part, artists don't have the same liberty as label execs; a deal that offers tens of thousands of dollars up front is life-altering bread for someone who's never seen that much money in one place before. But let's be honest: to some extent, artists know what they are getting into and sign up anyway, and labels aren't always looking to exploit and prey on young, naive artists. The game is unfair, but artists still sign record deals. It's not until years later, when albums like *3 Feet High* or *De La Soul Is Dead* blow up and shift culture, that the deal becomes obsolete. To a lesser degree at other labels, the artist and album don't have to change life; it's landing a top review or higher-than-expected stream count that validates work that should've gotten internal support from the jump. This notion of the starving artist needs to stop. That we romanticize artists' struggle only exacerbates the chasm between musicians and record execs and keeps wages and profit splits woefully uneven.

I'M NOT SURE THE EXACT MOMENT WHEN THE TRUST DISSOLVED BETWEEN De La and Tommy Boy. The easy answer is when the two sides started pointing fingers regarding the Turtles sample in '89, or when the band grew tired of seeing those damn daisies everywhere. Regardless, theirs is a cautionary tale of what can happen when both parties let tensions fester, leading to wounds that never heal. When neither side takes initiative to establish a healthy working relationship, you get blowups like this one. You get a group like De La trying to fight the system, and the system trying to maintain its dominance over the music.

De La's story isn't dissimilar to those of others in the industry who make pennies from their recorded work and earn the most money on the road. Yet in the 2020s, that wasn't so easy: the Covid-19 pandemic shut down the global economy and made it impossible to tour. Also, Dave wrestled with health issues—congestive heart failure—and couldn't travel that often anymore. Now in his fifties, he was still the same lighthearted person he'd always been, but his having to stay grounded made things feel uncertain.

The public pressure forced Tommy Boy to postpone the streaming release of De La's catalog and go back to negotiate with them. Finally, in August 2019, after seven months of going back and forth with the label, De La decided to end their relationship with Tommy. The label wouldn't give De La back their masters. In turn, citing "so many years of disappointment," the group said they didn't trust Tommy Boy and asked fans to not stream or buy physical records if they saw them in stores. It seemed they lost the fight and would continue without having their catalog up.

But then, in 2021, Tom Silverman sold the label to the independent music company Reservoir Media for $100 million, reopening the door for De La to get the rights to their work and have the catalog stream legally online. With support from Reservoir, the band hired Deborah Mannis-Gardner, who's known as something of a sample guru in rap, who combed through the band's first six albums in painstaking detail, excavating every sample to double-check it. It took over a year to vet every clip and get in touch with all the copyright holders. For the samples that couldn't be cleared, De La dusted off old equipment they've had for thirty years and re-created subtle drum breaks and bass lines and excised recognizable samples from other tracks.

The waiting game was the toughest part. Getting word that the music was coming, then having to be patient, was hard. On the one hand, I wanted to give the band enough time and grace to pull everything together, as clearing all those samples and setting up merch must have required boundless energy. Of course I wanted De La to get everything right, to not repeat history, but the glory felt so close for the guys. At last, after all the years of combat, of tussling with the label over one thing or another, after all the internal stress that comes with coalescing ideas and recording albums, the light was about to shine on the brothers from Long Island and their longtime followers.

So yes, De La, go away and come back when you're ready, when the music is ready, when the vinyl, cassettes, hoodies, and T-shirts are ready and—hopefully—a new album is ready. We'll be here ready as well, ready to throw rap hands at the show, to scrunch our faces at the unrelenting funk of "Oooh." and the triumphant wail of "Stakes Is High." We'll smile as if we know you personally and give the proper respect to you for giving so much to pop culture. We'll give you figurative flowers for illuminating our lives. We'll be there ready to test our headphones and car speakers with the blunted magnum force of "Plug Tunin'," "Tread Water" (you know, the frog song), and "De La Orgee" (you know, the awkward sex song) because, well, we love De La Soul. But man, I also wanted them to hurry up. Black men in their fifties don't always live to see triumph.

In a short time in late 2020 and 2021, we lost a number of cornerstone actors and rappers well before their time. These brothers passing in their fifties made me wonder what was going on, why we can't live to see old age and live long, healthy lives. At this point in my life, as a Black fortysomething with gray hair and a noisy hip that I sometimes think about replacing, death stops me cold and makes me second-guess my own choices. It also makes me consider my own clock. No one knows how they're gonna go or if it'll be tomorrow or sometime way down the line, but Black men—and Black people in general—don't get to consider mortality and shrug it off quickly. Each death sat me down and forced me to consider the inevitable: Will I live to see fifty? And if I make it there, how much longer do I have beyond that?

The sad reality is that some rappers don't age gracefully—not in the "You're too old, beat it, pops" way that some kids treat the OGs, but for some mysterious reason, they don't live well past fifty. And when we're not dying of natural causes, we're being killed by law enforcement. It's a slow burn that brings a palpable fatigue. I was happy for De La, yet sad that it had to take so long for them to resolve their business.

Somewhere along the way, I'd become an OG myself. I don't feel old, but within the scope of music journalism—where many writers and artists are ten to fifteen years younger than me—I guess the description makes sense. Somehow, I'd grown up with De La Soul's music and had been around long enough to see the band's life cycle. I'd been so used to growing up that it's wild to be a grown-up. I'd spent so much time being amazed by the band that I couldn't fathom the amazement being over.

The wonderment isn't done—every time I play *3 Feet High and Rising*, I'm transported back to simpler times, when the most serious item on my docket was whether or not the basketball court was too damp to play on. I still think of *Buhloone Mindstate* and my awkward transition through middle school. This was the music of my youth, and, no matter what else emerged, the foundation of all the esoteric music I liked as an adult can be traced back to Pos, Dave, and Maseo and the high bar they set all those years ago. I just put my head down and kept living, kept going to school and kept working; one day I look up and I'm putting younger people onto the music that helped shape me. The dynamic is jarring and beautiful, a solemn reminder of getting older commingled with the privilege of doing so. But growing up with De La never felt arduous, and it never felt like time was moving at all. And it's not until I got older and listened with middle-aged ears that I fully understood their magic: by being so timeless and ageless, they could still connect with fans from way back and newbies who'd heard about the band from longtimers like me.

THOUGH DAVE HAD BEEN FIERCELY PRIVATE, HE WAS OPEN ABOUT THE congestive heart failure he'd been suffering from. In the beginning of the video for "Royalty Capes," a single from *and the Anonymous Nobody . . .* , he told the camera from his home in Prince George's County, Maryland, that one day he fell asleep standing at his refrigerator for an hour and a half. He went to his doctor and learned that it was indeed a symptom of congestive heart failure and that he would need to wear a life vest to stay alive. "It'll shock me, and hopefully bring me back from the Matrix," Dave said, his face surprisingly laid-back for someone talking about such a thing. "I'm ready just to get to the stage. I miss it. I love traveling. I love being around my guys, and I want that back." Off and on over the next seven years, you'd see him in the occasional IG post, sometimes looking noticeably thinner and more weathered than he had been. Trips back and forth to the hospital ensued, but he never lost his trademark sarcasm. "New day received," read a caption in March 2021. "PS. It's simply a b&w photo, I'm not dead yet Inshallah." Even in his low moments, Dave had this way of making you feel at ease, of letting you know that it's gonna be OK, even if it's not. In his work and real life, his relaxed demeanor was almost disarming, and I could see why fans simply wanted to be in his presence.

I never took Dave's diagnosis seriously. Not that it wasn't serious, but Dave had always been there. I assumed he'd manage it and get better. Even in early February 2023, when Dave wasn't onstage rapping with Pos during a massive hip-hop tribute at the Grammys, I shrugged it off. I figured he was on the mend and simply couldn't make the trek to do the gig. So I was gutted—absolutely floored—when, a week later on February 12, 2023, news got out that Dave had died. I received word from a friend of mine, who texted a link to an *AllHipHop* story that announced his death as an exclusive. I was in denial. To be frank, the site wasn't exactly the go-to source for music journalism, so there was a part of me that wanted to get confirmation elsewhere. I went to IG. Questlove would know; let me see if he has a post up. Nothing. Maybe NPR? *Pitchfork? Okayplayer?* Nothing at those places just yet. An email to De La's manager went unreturned. It wasn't until a press release came through from the band's longtime publicist, Tony Ferguson, that the reality set in: Dave was dead at the age of fifty-four.

While every celebrity death hits me differently, this one had an impact I couldn't quite fathom. I'd been working on this book for roughly three years, so I was deeply embedded in the De La universe. I'd been poring through every song, every verse, every album. Dave's voice had been ringing in my ears. Every memory associated with my upbringing through De La came rushing to the fore. For the next three days, I tried to put pen to paper, but I was overcome with grief. I found myself walking around in a fog. As a journalist who used to cover crime and politics, I thought I'd developed calluses from seeing all this despair. You take death and hopelessness as a part of the gig and become jaded to what the job presents. Old-school journalists were taught to play it down the middle, to not show emotion, to lock those feelings away and get the work done. As I've gotten older, I can no longer ignore such emotions, especially when it comes to those I've spoken to or whose music has had a profound force on my life.

So with Dave, I leaned into the grief. I sat with it. Part of my youth had died, and along with it part of my innocence. Dave was not only the heartbeat of De La Soul; he was the heartbeat of the style of rap I grew up idolizing. Today we're all in a hurry to go nowhere in particular. We scroll for news and hot takes, looking for the next dopamine hit. When death arises, we post grainy photos, old performance videos, and short remembrances meant to express our respective sadness. It's all "RIP to the homie," "Rest well," and "Fly high," but do we really stop and reflect on what these people mean to us? Do we mourn, or is it a rush to see who can be the deepest and most sincere? And we're not allowed to sit there long, our grief interrupted by some other tragedy vying for attention. The clock needs to stop when our legends leave, but in a world of constant sorrow and disconnection, is that even possible anymore?

I was angry. Why did Tommy Boy take so long? If they would've done good business from the jump, maybe Dave would've seen the fruits of his labor, the "more land" he once sought. If this situation could've been resolved while Dave was in his thirties or forties, perhaps his story would've played out differently. That's how my irrational fan brain thought. Then I realized shit just happens. You can't predict death. It was a sad coincidence I had to reckon with, no matter how much I wanted to blame the record label and lament the fragility of human existence.

Pos and Maseo faced a similar struggle in early March. The band's music was coming back to streaming on the third, to coincide with the original release date of *3 Feet High and Rising*. There was press to be done and a tour on the horizon. Those things just couldn't be halted. The saddest part was that Dave's passing came as new plans were falling into place for the group. Instead of the trio taking a victory lap as one of rap's national treasures, they had to publicly mourn while putting on brave faces. If I was devastated by Dave's passing, I can't imagine what those brothers went through. He was their dear friend and collaborator. He was family. They shared hotel rooms and tour buses, laughter, anger, and disagreements. They fought the system together, supporting each other through the highs and lows. "A true artist who used music to inspire and uplift others," Pos wrote about Dave. "As we attempt to navigate this world without you, we stand grateful and proud of all you accomplished on this earth." It was crazy to envision a landscape without Dave in it.

Undeterred, Pos and Maseo went through with a massive De La celebration at Webster Hall in Manhattan that featured just about everyone that the band touched over the years: Common, Queen Latifah, Busta Rhymes, Large Professor, Monie Love, Dave Chappelle. Featuring DJ sets by Stretch Armstrong and D-Nice and brief performances by some of the aforementioned MCs, it felt like a proper homage to a band that inspired so many. It was scattered and playful. At times it looked like there were more people onstage than in the audience. Right there in one place was my childhood and young adulthood, and now—as an older fan— they were contemporaries. That's the beauty of hip-hop culture: if you're in it, you're all the way in, whether you're a writer, an MC, a DJ, or a photographer. It pulls you in and shows love if you're well-meaning and respectful to it. Those who love it do so fiercely, doing what they can to preserve and document. Whether or not you see someone on TV doesn't—or shouldn't—matter. Many of the people in the room and watching the livestream cared deeply about what was happening there and felt a part of what occurred. At the center of all this was Pos and Maseo, center stage and emotionally delicate. Mase told the story of his moving to Long Island in 1984 and how he had to retool his thinking once he landed in the suburbs. "I thought I was moving further away from my dream," he said. "But God knew I was moving closer to it."

God's plan is real—for those who believe in such things, of course. We can push and plan for our lives to go a certain way, but events happen for a reason, sometimes beyond comprehension or understanding. Who would've known that three quirky cats would meet around the way, have the same sensibilities and work ethic, and set out on a distinctive course that would shift the course of hip-hop forever? Why was it destined for them to do it? Seeing all those legends in Webster Hall made me reckon not only with De La's legacy but with that of everyone in the group's orbit.

It made me wonder if we ever truly appreciate Black genius or if we're resigned to just let it fade away in pursuit of something younger. At what point do we give the JBs their due flowers? Monie Love and the like? Death makes you reckon with the mark you're leaving on the world. And seeing De La and their friends onstage made me happy they were finally getting love, but it made me realize that the collective hasn't been loved enough.

The work of Jungle Brothers, then De La, blossomed into this vast collective of hip-hop culture that's still being felt across broad subdivisions of Black creativity, guided by the promise of inspiring other artists to push boundaries and create their own communities. Over the years, you'd hear people whispering about their love of De La while offering effusive praise for other acts. But for the first time I could remember, the adoration was tangible, palpable, concentrated right there for the world to see and feel. It was a shame that it took death and a Herculean fight with Tommy Boy to arrive at this moment, but it was satisfying to see De La getting their proper credit. "I am truly thankful for all of you who are here," Pos told the crowd. "You best believe that my nigga Dave is looking down right now on everybody."

IT ONLY TOOK DE LA THIRTY YEARS TO WIN, WHICH I GUESS MAKES SENSE when taking their career in totality. They've always been a slow and steady, unhurried presence. Never tantalized by fame. In my own career I've fallen asleep wondering when I'll stop being underrated as a writer and thinker, wondering when I'll get the glory that seems to touch everyone else so easily. De La offered me a lesson in humility: stay the course, keep experimenting, and your time will come. If it doesn't? Well, at least you pushed some dope art into the world and impacted culture as best as possible. Worrying about what everyone else is doing only damages your own mental health, creating a false sense of failure. Indirectly, De La was saying, "Don't worry about that other shit. Do you." To this day, their music reminds me to follow my heart, no matter how bizarre or outlandish it might skew. In a genre where rappers compete over who has the flyest clothes and cars, De La eschewed such grandeur in search of what was meaningful and resonant, art that didn't give in to trends. Whether or not you actively listened to De La's music, it's woven into the tapestry of pop culture and has influenced your fave's fave. People are coming back around to them, because hip-hop isn't so hard-rock or serious now, and it's more acceptable to express yourself without fear of being labeled soft.

When I think of De La, I think of my family. I see the weathered photos of my aunts and grandparents; I hear the band's songs tumbling through big speakers, pouring from dilapidated cars, glowing through my sixteen-inch TV with no bass in it at all. I think of the friends I've lost, their laughter still so prominent and so visceral. I think of how I felt when I lost them, how the grief reignites with each play of "Trying People." I think of ubiquity, the language of the Inner Sound or the Ill Shit and how it cuts through the din.

To grow up with De La is to grow up precariously, not knowing where you stand socially while keeping comfortable there. It's understanding you're different, that what you're into might be considered peculiar until everyone else is doing it. It's standing to the side and waiting for y'all to discover it, to recognize that's where true artistry lives. Being a De La fan means being a fan of the unknown and unforeseen and embracing the high-wire act that typifies them. But it always made for greater rewards. De La is freedom, unabashed Blackness in all its different levels and layers. Being a fan meant you can be that too. In the spirit of Funkadelic, Sly and the Family Stone, and *Star Trek*, De La ignited a mass of kids without an artistic epicenter. As older men, they still felt like those same nineteen-year-olds trying to stand out, trying to exist on their own terms, still unsure of the grand magnitude they possessed.

Even now, as bona fide legends, they seem unsure of their footing, almost in awe of their powers and ashamed of their mistakes. And even at Webster Hall, they didn't look especially comfortable, but they knew they had to be there—for us, for Dave, for hip-hop. In essence, that's what being a De La devotee means—to be near the spotlight but never directly in it, to want to be loved but also craving your solitude, to be thrust into the light by loved ones who see more in you than you see in yourself. It's being gracious enough to embrace the cherishing and spread the same love to others.

Growing up with De La meant not growing up at all, really. It's being mature beyond your years but also childish enough to live joyously. It's doing adult shit before you're supposed to. It's the need for peace and reciprocity, the kudos you know you want but are afraid to ask for. It's feeling guilty for feeling that way. It's quiet self-assessment when the real talk goes out hot. It's getting older and understanding that flossy rappers made points too; that they can aspire to generational wealth and look good doing it. It's letting folks know you ain't no easy way. It's "Don't sleep on these hands, I'll beat yo' ass—respectfully." De La was, and continues to be, everything, a guiding light blazing a trail through the hereafter.

When I think of De La, I think of what would've happened if they weren't around. I marvel at how colorless it would've been, how aggressive or angry or violent, without the band's counterbalance. I wonder if hip-hop would even know what pastel colors looked like, and how perfect they looked against an equally bright floral garden. I wonder if we'd ever know who the Turtles are, or how good Hall and Oates sounds atop shakers and funk-centered drums. Would we have such patchwork production? Would we have A Tribe Called Quest's jazz-rap hybrid? Would Amityville have a claim to fame besides a scary house and a few horror films? I doubt the genre would be as open-minded, and I don't think rap would be as cheerful. In turn, I don't think we would have listeners equally indebted to the after-school science club, *Mike Tyson's Punch-Out!*, old Don Cherry records, and macking girls at the mall. Who knows if Prince Paul would have the name he does now without De La Soul as his creative outlet.

When I think of De La, I think of the Black pride they exuded, and how—perhaps indirectly—they instilled that same pride in everyone else. I think of Charlie Rock, who was there in the very beginning, how his name shouldn't be erased from the band's history. I think of Tommy Boy Records for giving the band a shot. As easy as it is to vilify the label, someone had to see something in De La and put the records out. I see the Gumby-style haircuts. I hear the New York accents and feel adolescent jealousy, wanting to be in the city but unable to be because I live four hours down 95 South. I think of the writer, poet, and musician Greg Tate, who famously said there was no such thing as alternative hip-hop. Then I thought about how there's no other way to describe De La, because it didn't sound like anything else. I think about how dumbfounded my friends can be when trying to dissect De La, how their heads drop and their hands wave about when trying to find the words. I think about how natural that is, how the band defies sensibility. I think how we look past the shortcomings, the songs that weren't good that we defended anyway. I think about how their path could've been easier if that damn sample was cleared. I think "Did they even need that song?" in bewilderment because it was just an interlude. Then I fall back, realizing that De La's story played out the way it was supposed to.

I think of the time I walked into the Beacon to see Wu-Tang Clan in 2019 and being shoulder to shoulder with De La, and how I was too scared to say anything to them. I had too much respect for them; this was De La Soul; it didn't seem real. I almost didn't believe they were there, walking among the crowd like they weren't who they were. I want to know how Pos and Maseo are truly doing in the wake of Dave's passing. I don't want the packaged interview answer with a publicist on the line; I want to hear how Kelvin and Vince are holding up. I want to know if, as Black people, they feel appreciated and seen, or if they feel pressure to be perfect and push their self-care to the rear. I'd want to tell them don't do that; that rest is vital and grieving hits when it hits. The music is why we're here, of course, but I wonder about them as humans. What's life like beyond all this? I wonder if they feel accomplished or if they're still pushing for the perfect album and what that sounds like. I think about aging and savoring the journey, about pushing toward the future without sacrificing the present.

I wonder why the Native Tongues never dropped an album, why they couldn't push egos aside and just do the damn thing. I wonder how it would've sounded to hear Pos, Q-Tip, and Queen Latifah going in on a track, or how Dave, Phife, and Dres would've coexisted in song.

Most of all, I'm grateful I grew up as hip-hop was growing up, that my coming of age dovetailed with De La's ascendance. I'm thankful to have seen the initial reactions to their work, to celebrate the milestones, to see it disappear and come back renewed. It's been thrilling to witness the "aha!" moment that washes over newer listeners just now getting into the catalog. That's got to be better than any record sale, positive review, or Grammy Award. The best any creator can do is craft something and hope someone engages with it. And that they're so moved that they tell someone else about it, so on and so forth.

It's been over thirty years since the release of De La's first album, and here we are still amazed by it, still peeling the onion, still trying to gather why it worked. The band proves that it's always best to color outside the lines, to take risks and live with the results. They're the purveyors of "Let's see": Let's see how this sounds; let's see how this looks; let's see about making our own way in the marketplace.

To hear De La is to hear brilliance, insolence, conceit, and kindness within the scope of one verse or one song and getting all the references as they land. It's understanding that what they did was limitless and prescient, even when their output wavered and a comeback felt unlikely. When I think of De La, I think of how they never broke up, which is a damn miracle in the music business. I see their masterful live show and how they pause and stutter the beat in certain spots. I see that one time that Maseo left the DJ booth, walked to the front of the stage, and barked at a patron to put his phone down and enjoy the show. I think of how great it was to see Pos rapping at the Grammys as a tribute to hip-hop culture.

When I think of De La, I think of resilience—the most important attribute any creator can have. I think of the kids who have yet to discover De La and how their worlds are going to open once they do. I think about the evermore, not just mine and not just De La's, but that of our culture, our people, our ancestors. I think about where Dave is and what he left behind, wondering if he knew how beloved he was before leaving this place. Then I listen to the band's music like it just came out, like I'm still that kid peeking over my cousin's turntable, still that teen doing laundry and tossing it wherever because Dave did it in that one video, still hunting for an original copy of *Stakes Is High* on the Internet, still shocked that their music is widely and easily shareable. De La Soul is everlasting. Immortality looks good on them.

EPILOGUE

Dave,

You didn't know me, but you were there with me the whole time, guiding me along with your dazzling wit and demeanor. I couldn't understand how you could be so cool and so unconventional, how you could sport the wildest hairstyle and throw garments together that seemingly didn't match. But then it all looked so effortless, so casual. I couldn't classify your lyrical style either. It was real talk yet not so straightforward, complex lattices that I had to read while your voice filtered through the stereo. It was conversational and theatrical; oftentimes, I didn't know what was being said or what it meant, but I had to keep listening. I had to try to dissect what you were conveying. Indirectly, you helped strengthen my cognition and ushered me into a deep love affair with music and a life of analyzing the written and spoken word.

Thanks to you, I prefer listening to that which isn't easily seen or comprehended, music that scrambles my brain a little. Elsewhere, you knew how to express what I was feeling. Right as hip-hop was becoming too sanitized for my liking, there you were in the "Stakes Is High" video talking about the weakened state of a culture we both loved so dearly. I didn't always know your language, but I wanted to be a part of it so I could laugh too.

When I think of you, I'm reminded of my cousin Eric.
How he used to cut hair like you cut Pos's and Maseo's hair. I
remember how he'd give me these ornate high-top fades with
parts on the side. I can't say it was solely because of you, but I
know that I'd seen you in the "Me Myself and I" video by then,
so maybe you were an indirect influence. You were synonymous
with '80s rap and fashion, and you embraced it with a shrug and
a grin—as if you belonged there the whole time. You seemed
like family, because you and my cousin were so much alike. You
were both gentle and carefree, free-ass people who did what
you wanted when you wanted. You were a trendsetter without
trying to be one, a voice prodding through Tribe's "Award
Tour" and Camp Lo's "B-Side to Hollywood." You came off
like a dude who had a pass in various circles: the hood and the
alt-rap scene, with punk rockers, folk cats, and jazz heads. You
were ubiquitous and nudged me to aspire to the same level of
omnipresence. I dug how you and your friends rewrote the rules
of Blackness in rap, how I never thought of you guys as soft.
Like my cousin, you were artsy and street, a brother comfortable
with himself.

Your passing unlocked a myriad of old memories and old
music, and I didn't know whether to smile, laugh, or cry when
running through it all. It felt like when Eric died in some
faraway town under mysterious circumstances. With my cousin,
I think I was just shocked. He'd always been around—swirling
through my head when I played EPMD, Ol' Dirty Bastard,
or Too $hort. It wasn't until I got older that I realized how
impactful he was—and, in turn, you were. The "Itsoweezee"
video made me want to go to that high school and say peace to
Pharoahe Monch and Lords of the Underground. That was wild
because school wasn't always my jam. By then I had to think
about how the rest of my life would look, and that sometimes

felt like a bit much because I was somewhat intimidated by the enormity of it all. But when I saw you floating through the video in a tan bucket hat and green Native Tongues T-shirt, it made education look cool (though there wasn't much learning going on in the clip). You were always the calm center between Pos's raw emotion and Maseo's fire.

Man, how could you be so collected in this game? Were there times when you felt hurt? Misunderstood? Tired of it all? You encouraged me to be a better writer, to take my craft seriously but not be so buttoned-up and rigid about it. You taught me this: as long as my heart is on the page, the work's going to go where it's supposed to go. You taught me not to seek validation from strangers. You made me wonder what, or who, pissed you off on "Verbal Clap," because I'd never heard you spit that hard before.

Your passing makes me think of another Dave, my neighbor who I often see downstairs. We'd never talked about you specifically, but you were just that universal. You were meditative, and your words were counterpunches to the misogyny of other rappers. Though you spoke to masses of people, your words stemmed from the love and protection of Black people and Black culture.

Your death came six months before my mother, Delores, died. And I'm sitting here now trying to reconcile her passing, wondering where she is in the universe. Nothing prepares you for the day you become the parent, when you suddenly have to feed your mom and speak to doctors on her behalf. Nothing prepares you for the evening call from the hospital to approve or deny a do-not-resuscitate order, or to watch your mom become disoriented and stop eating. Nothing prepares you for getting her home for hospice care, then walking upstairs just as she's taking her last breaths. There's no shaking the helplessness, seeing her struggle to breathe, knowing that she's leaving. Then having to plan her memorial just a week after her baby sister—my aunt Claudette—died. But when I close my eyes, I envision my mom somewhere happy, running through the garden she used to as a child, no longer in pain or distress. I also can't shake how I saw her in those final moments. I think there's something to be said about mother-son intuition, that I thought to check on her *right* as she transitioned. I'm devastated and will be for some time, racked with grief yet with profound moments of happiness.

What can be said once doctors tell you she's no longer responding to the medicine, that it's best to focus on comfort over recovery? How does one reconcile the demise of such cherished loved ones? How do you let the grief reside without it taking over? How can I mourn and be practical? How do I sit with the pain without the guilt of moving on? What do you do when your closest family member is suddenly gone? I commend and feel for Pos and Maseo, because they have to soldier through grief publicly. I did so somewhat privately without thousands of people watching.

I bet my mom could appreciate what you guys represented. She was a fan of good music of all eras and genres, whether it was Al Green or Elton John, Bon Iver or James Blake. I can see her nodding to "Sunshine" or moving her shoulders to "Me Myself and I." She helped shape my cultural perspective by letting me explore. Where other parents might shy away from hip-hop because of a few bad words, Mom let me discover what the D.A.I.S.Y. Age was all about. She let my cousin Eric give me a wild high-top fade like you had. She knew that kids would be kids and her job was to keep me on the right path. Now that she's gone, I keep her lessons with me. She would want me to live abundantly without limitations. To do what I was put here to do.

I still struggle with my place in the world. Because I don't fit into most boxes, I often feel like a loner in this cliqued-up industry. But, Dave, through your spirit and your rhymes, you tell me to stay the course. I don't know how to feel about your absence, though even in silence, I can still hear your baritone cutting through the drum, and I can still see you standing there—onstage and in the videos, commanding the set from your elevated perch.

You are one of the baddest rappers to ever do it.

You are appreciated and you are missed, and I pray you continue to fly. To Mom: You are my heart and soul. I see you, the full you, the caretaker, the provider, the connoisseur of stand-up comedy, the lover of all things artful. I pray that my tears on earth don't keep you from happiness in the hereafter. To Claudette: I remain inspired by your honesty and free-spirited nature. I thank you for being so open and so fun, and for peppering my childhood with great music and laughter. To Dave, Mom, Claudette, my grandparents, friends, and other loved ones who have become ancestors: I love and admire you all.

From my heart to your soul,
Marcus

ACKNOWLEDGMENTS

Reading liner notes as a child, I used to roll my eyes at rappers who wrote "You know who you are" in their acknowledgments. Now as an adult with a shifting friends and family list, and with two books to my credit, I'll say this:

Sincerest thanks to all the loved ones in my life who helped make *High and Rising* possible. You know who you are, and I'll be thanking you personally.

Publicly, though, I want to thank De La Soul for everything they've given to hip-hop culture. On behalf of all the left-of-center kids who were deemed cool but different, I thank them for making us feel comfortable in our respective skin. I hope this offering—as historical, critical, honest and loving as it is—lands with them and music fans in some form or fashion.

As I've said repeatedly over the years, it's important to honor Black creators while they're here to bask in the love. And it's especially important to do this in the literary space for future generations to see. De La Soul, like Kendrick Lamar in my previous book, is just as vital as anyone in rock, pop, and classical genres.

Thanks to all the artists who keep it weird and interesting, who aren't afraid to take bold creative risks in public.

Let's keep breaking the mold.

With love,
MJM

NOTES

PROLOGUE

xiii **"I appreciate how and why it happened"** OneAdmin, "De La Soul: 'Three Black Men Staying Together for So Long Is Beautiful and Important,'" 107.1 K-HITS website, June 7, 2022, https://www.khitsboise.com/2022/06/07/de-la-soul-three-black-men-staying-together-for-so-long-is-beautiful-and-important/.

xv **"a longer term for theft"** Steve Hochman, "Judge Raps Practice of 'Sampling,'" *Los Angeles Times*, December 18, 1991, https://www.latimes.com/archives/la-xpm-1991-12-18-ca-617-story.html.

xvi **"We would've just left it off"** Mass Appeal, prod., *De La Soul Is Not Dead*, on YouTube at https://www.youtube.com/watch?v=8i346sS-_8Q.

xvi **"we followed all the requirements"** Maseo, interview at Red Bull Music Academy, 2012, https://www.redbullmusicacademy.com/lectures/maseo.

CHAPTER 1: FROM STRONG ISLAND, WITH LOVE

4 **"clutter of everyone living on top of one another"** Ed Power, "Three Feet High and Still Rising," *Irish Examiner*, July 23, 2013, https://www.irishexaminer.com/lifestyle/arid-20237625.html.

5 **"We had this crazy landlord".** J Nicely and Sebastian Demian, "Say No Go," *Frank151*, January 27, 2012.

6 **"a cassette they had with someone rhyming on it"** Kyle Eustice, "The Right Stuff," *Wax Poetics* 55, Summer 2013.

8 **"When I saw G Rap at a party"** Maseo, interview at Red Bull Music Academy, 2012, https://www.redbullmusicacademy.com/lectures/maseo.

9 **"'In my house, you better eat up everything on your plate'"** Preezy Brown, "9 Gems from De La Soul's 'Drink Champs' Episode," Revolt, March 29, 2019.

9 **"I eat it a lot"** De La Soul, "De La Soul Speaks," 1989 electronic press kit on YouTube at https://www.youtube.com/watch?v=wim7wgmhZYc.

9 **"It was wack"** Maseo, interview at Red Bull Music Academy, 2012.

11 **"'This is horrible'"** Adam Pasulka, "Royal Family," *Frank151*, January 27, 2012, 52.

11 **"It was dope, but it dragged"** Open Mike Eagle, "Prince Paul talks meeting De La Soul for the first time…," July 9, 2020, on YouTube at https://www.youtube.com/watch?v=E1ktz091GZw.

11 **"The first thing he said out the gate"** Maseo, interview at Red Bull Music Academy, 2012.

12 **"He became pretty obnoxious"** Maseo, interview at Red Bull Music Academy, 2012.

14 **"I was in the mix, like, 'No, do it over'"** Adam Pasulka, "Royal Family," 55.

15 **"'Yes. We need to do this'"** Justin Briggs, "Tommy's Boys," *Frank151*, January 27, 2012, 29.

17 **"Hall's voice over a Sly and the Family Stone record"** Dave Simpson. "How We Made *3 Feet High and Rising*," *Guardian*, April 29, 2014, https://www.theguardian.com/music/2014/apr/29/how-we-made-3-feet-high-and-rising-de-la-soul.

17 **"It was playful, childlike and fun"** Simpson, "How We Made *3 Feet High and Rising*."

18 **"We had something else to say"** Evan Serpick, "*3 Feet High and Rising*: De La Soul's Track by Track Guide to Groundbreaking 1989 LP," *Rolling Stone*, June 3, 2009, https://www.rollingstone.com/feature/de-la-soul-1989-lp-3-feet-high-rising-track-by-track-guide-69292/.

19 **"Even if he thought what we were doing was stupid or crazy"** Angus Batey, "Magic Number: The Story of *3 Feet High and Rising*," *Quietus*, March 4, 2019, https://thequietus.com/articles/26140-de-la-soul-3-feet-high-and-rising-review-anniversary

19 **"sitting around listening to stuff"** Batey, "Magic Number: The Story of *3 Feet High and Rising*."

22 **"Nothing if not zany"** Michael Azerrad, "Review: *3 Feet High and Rising*," *Rolling Stone*, March 23, 1989, https://www.rollingstone.com/music/music-album-reviews/3-feet-high-and-rising-95814/.

22 **"radically unlike any rap you or anybody else has ever heard"** Robert Christgau, "De La Soul," robertchristgau.com, https://www.robertchristgau.com/get_artist.php?id=337.

22 **"sounded like those tapes you made when you were a little kid"** Batey, "Magic Number: The Story of 3 Feet High and Rising."

23 **"I never really liked that record"** Serpick, "*3 Feet High and Rising*: De La Soul's Track by Track Guide to Groundbreaking 1989 LP."

23 **"We actually sat down in Paul's room and came up with that idea"** Serpick "*3 Feet High and Rising*: De La Soul's Track by Track Guide to Groundbreaking 1989 LP."

26 **"We put every idea that we had into that record"** Wade Sheridan, "Beastie Boys talk hip-hop, *Paul's Boutique* on Tonight Show," UPI, April 10, 2020, https://www.upi.com/Entertainment_News/TV/2020/04/10/Beastie-Boys -talk-hip-hop-Pauls-Boutique-on-Tonight-Show/2481586520101/.

CHAPTER 2: OTHERS FROM THE BROTHER PLANET

31 **"It was cool, pretty funny, and original"** Dante Ross, "Rap De Rap Show," *Frank151*, January 27, 2012, 42.

32 **"we had to suck it up and get our show right"** Dante Ross, "Rap De Rap Show," 41.

34 **"I'd be like, 'Yo, did this really happen?'"** Mass Appeal, prod., *De La Soul Is Not Dead*, on YouTube at https://www.youtube.com/watch?v=8i346sS-_8Q.

35 **more white people started rapping** *Record Collector*, "De La Soul," April 15, 2019, https://recordcollectormag.com/articles/de-la-soul.

40 **"We just started dying laughing"** Rob Kenner, "When a Daisy Grows in Your Mind," *VIBE*, March 4, 2023, https://www.vibe.com/features/editorial/a -daisy-for-dave-trugoy-the-dove-1234739889/.

CHAPTER 3: A CLASSIC FOUND IN THE GARBAGE

44 **"They're beating people up"** Open Mike Eagle, *What Had Happened Was*, August 5, 2020.

44 **"It's all about dying and being rejuvenated as something else"** Steven Daly, *SPIN*, May 1991, 54.

46 **"Overall"** J Nicely and Sebastian Demian, "Say No Go," *Frank151*, January 27, 2012, 148.

47 **"Looking back on it"** Nicely and Demian, "Say No Go."

49 **"It brings out a feeling of letting yourself go on the weekend"** ATCO, "Record Report: *De La Soul Is Dead*," *The Source*, May 1991, https://ifihavent .wordpress.com/2007/04/20/classic-review-de-la-soul-is-dead-in-the-source -1991/.

49 **In a positive four-star review** Scott Poulson-Bryant, "De La Soul Is Dead," *Rolling Stone*, May 30, 1991, https://www.rollingstone.com/music/music-- album-reviews/de-la-soul-is-dead-250816/.

56 **It's "musical collage"** Frank Owen, "Bite This: Our 1989 Feature on Sampling," *SPIN*, May 9, 2021. https://www.spin.com/2021/05/bite-this-1989 -sampling-feature/.

CHAPTER 4: WHEN LIFE IMITATES ART (OR VICE VERSA?)

61 **"It was a load of bullshit"** Mark van Schaick, Tim Goodyer, "De La Soul," *Music Technology*, 1992.

62 **"If you asked me whether the new CD has been received"** Van Schaick, Goodyer, "De La Soul."

67 **"What once made De La Soul special"** Karen Schoemer "Review/Rap; De La Soul's New Image: Toughness," *New York Times*, February 18, 1992.

69 **"I grew up on them dudes"** Reyan Ali, "Madlib Muses on Methods Behind His Madness," *SPIN*, March 20, 2014, https://www.spin.com/2014/03/madlib -freddie-gibbs-pinata-interview/.

70 **"Rap records always had some dialogue in them"** Jeff Weiss, "A History of the Hip Hop Skit," *Red Bull Music Academy Daily*, July 7, 2015, https://daily .redbullmusicacademy.com/2015/07/hip-hop-skits-history.

71 **"After we finished recording"** Weiss, "A History of the Hip Hop Skit."

CHAPTER 5: GETTIN' GROWN

78 **"We made demos together and I thought he was an amazing lyricist"** Todd Gilchrist, "How Gravediggaz Made a Gruesome Hip-Hop Masterpiece," *Entertainment Weekly*, August 9, 2019, https://ew.com/music/2019/08/09 /gravediggaz-6-feet-deep-anniversary/.

81 **"[It's] about how I felt"** Paul Meara, "De La Soul Explains Early Native Tongues Tension," *HipHopDX*, June 14, 2015, https://hiphopdx.com/news/id .34252/title.de-la-soul-explains-early-native-tongues-tension.

87 **"We had been through the 'machine'"** Oliver Wang, "20 Years Ago, De La Soul Refused to Go Pop," *NPR*, December 30, 2013, https://www.wbur.org /npr/258155415/20-years-ago-de-la-soul-refused-to-go-pop.

88 **Stanley Crouch** Robert Wilkins, "Miles Davis: 'The Most Brilliant Sellout in the History of Jazz,'" *WhatNext Journal*, https://www.whatnextjournal.org.uk /Pages/Back/Wnext22/Miles.html.

89 **"firmly on the path of the sellout"** Stanley Crouch, "Miles: The Autobiography, by Miles Davis and Quincy Troupe," February 12, 1990.

89 They **"felt a flow"** Oliver Wang, "20 Years Ago, De La Soul Refused to Go Pop," *NPR*, December 30, 2013, https://www.npr.org/sections/therecord/2013 /12/30/258155415/20-years-ago-de-la-soul-refused-to-go-pop.

90 **"wasn't really doing what we needed it to do"** *Okayplayer*, "De La Soul Reveals the Secret History of *Stakes Is High*," January 5, 2023, https://www.okayplayer .com/originals/de-la-soul-stakes-is-high.html.

90 **In an October 1993 review** Greg Tate, "Recordings View; They Go Where Few Rappers Dare to Follow," *New York Times*, October 17, 1993, https:// www.nytimes.com/1993/10/17/archives/recordings-view-they-go-where-few -rappers-dare-to-follow.html.

90 **In *Entertainment Weekly*** James Bernard, "*Buhloone Mindstate*," *Entertainment Weekly*, October 8, 1993, https://ew.com/article/1993/10/08/buhloone-mindstate/.

90 **"I didn't really get it'"** Wang, "20 Years Ago, De La Soul Refused to Go Pop."

92 **"I think we were just a little too creative"** "De La Soul: Still Grinding," *AllHipHop.com*, January 1, 2005, https://allhiphop.com/features/de-la-soul-still -grinding/.

CHAPTER 6: FROM LANDOVER WITH LOVE

108 **"Taking the seat of being the producers"** Victoria Hernandez, "De La Soul Explains Who Is Carrying *Stakes Is High* Legacy on 20th Anniversary of Album," *HipHopDX*, July 1, 2016, https://hiphopdx.com/news/id.39452 /title.de-la-soul-explains-who-is-carrying-stakes-is-high-legacy-on-20th -anniversary-of-album.

109 **"We were just trying to think about"** *Okayplayer*, "De La Soul Reveals the Secret History of *Stakes Is High*," January 5, 2023, https://www.okayplayer.com /originals/de-la-soul-stakes-is-high.html.

112 **"It was rough"** *Okayplayer*, "De La Soul Reveals the Secret History of *Stakes Is High*."

CHAPTER 7: WHERE WERE YOU THE FIRST TIME YOU HEARD *STAKES IS HIGH*?

118 **"I was just trying to say to someone"** *Okayplayer*, "De La Soul Reveals The Secret History of *Stakes Is High*," January 5, 2023, https://www.okayplayer .com/originals/de-la-soul-stakes-is-high.html.

119 **"There was definitely a misunderstanding that turned into a rift"** *Okayplayer*, "De La Soul Reveals The Secret History of *Stakes Is High*."

119 **"most of the 17 pieces on *Stakes Is High*"** David Sprague, *Rolling Stone*, August 8, 1996.

119 **Calling it "cranky"** Jeff Salamon, "*Stakes Is High*," *SPIN*, August 1996, 96.

120 **"Hip-hop's trippiest trio take an unfortunate turn"** Ethan Smith, "*Stakes Is High*," *Entertainment Weekly*, July 12, 1996.

122 **"I get tired of certain MCs"** "De La Soul Rap City Interview '96 Talking *Stakes Is High*," a 1996 interview on YouTube at https://www.youtube.com /watch?v=CGStQE3Ns3U.

123 **"We've been blessed to be three individuals"** Stereo Williams, "De La Soul's Return: The Alternative Hip-Hop Legends Are Still Keeping It Weird," *The Daily Beast*, April 14, 2015, https://www.thedailybeast.com/de-la-souls-return -the-alternative-hip-hop-legends-are-still-keeping-it-weird.

132 **told to Joe Clair in an interview** "De La Soul Rap City Interview '96 Talking *Stakes Is High*."

132 **as *Slate* put it** Jack Hamilton, "When I First Heard *Stakes Is High*," *Slate*, July 20, 2016, https://slate.com/culture/2016/07/de-la-soul-stakes-is-high-and-hip -hops-nostalgia-problem.html.

CHAPTER 8: LIFE WITHOUT DE LA

136 **a flash point in the battle** Miles Marshall Lewis, "All About the Benjamins," *LA Weekly*, March 25, 1998, https://www.laweekly.com/all-about-the-benjamins/.

139 **"We really don't have a fear of that 'out of sight, out of mind' thing"** Richard Harrington, *Washington Post*, July 20, 2000, https://www.washingtonpost .com/archive/lifestyle/2000/07/21/spotlight/6d7c759e-0a93-4fb2-a25a -63ce471ec9ed/.

141 *"Mosaic Thump* **is definitely a chorus-driven record"** Harrington, *Washington Post.*

154 **"We're going to return to the foundation"** Billboard Staff, "Tommy Boy Artists Dance Again," *Billboard*, March 11, 2002, https://www.billboard.com /music/music-news/tommy-boy-artists-dance-again-76511/.

154 **"We feel very happy honestly"** Grouchy Greg Watkins, "AHH Exclusive: De La Soul Leave Tommy Boy to Elektra," *AllHipHop.com*, March 7, 2002, https:// allhiphop.com/news/ahh-exclusive-de-la-soul-leave-tommy-boy-to-elektra/.

CHAPTER 9: A CATALOG ALMOST LOST TO TIME

158 **according to the economist Joel Waldfogel** Joel Waldfogel, "Music Piracy and Its Effects on Demand, Supply, and Welfare," Carlson School and Department of Economics, University of Minnesota, and NBER, https://www .journals.uchicago.edu/doi/full/10.1086/663157.

158 **"Our contracts on those early albums"** Emma Saunders, "De La Soul: Classic Back Catalogue Finally Available for Streaming," *BBC*, January 3, 2023, https://www.bbc.com/news/entertainment-arts-64152051.

162 **"We thought that would be the best gift after twenty-five years"** "An Interview with De La Soul's Dave Jude Jolicoeur, a.k.a. Trugoy the Dove," *Kickstarter*, August 26, 2016, https://medium.com/kickstarter/an-interview -with-de-la-souls-dave-jude-jolicoeur-a-k-a-trugoy-the-dove-3df50d48d3b.

169 **as Pos told** *Rolling Stone* **in 2014** Jason Newman, "De La Soul to Make Entire Catalog Available for Free," *Rolling Stone*, February 13, 2014, https:// www.rollingstone.com/music/music-news/de-la-soul-to-make-entire-catalog -available-for-free-70568/.

169 **"Everything is redundant"** Patrick Flanary, "De La Soul Blast 'Redundant' Hip-Hop with First Single Since 2004," *Rolling Stone*, April 4, 2013, https:// www.rollingstone.com/music/music-news/de-la-soul-blast-redundant-hip-hop -with-first-single-since-2004-172028/.

171 **"There were definitely labels interested in De La Soul"** Joe Coscarelli, "De La Soul's Kickstarter Campaign Raises $600,874," *New York Times*, May 5, 2015, https://www.nytimes.com/2015/05/06/arts/music/de-la-souls-kickstarter -campaign-raises-600874.html.

173 **Where** *SPIN* **awarded** SPIN Staff, "Review: De La Soul, Still Rising After All These Years on 'and the Anonymous Nobody…,'" *SPIN*, August 22, 2016, https:// www.spin.com/2016/08/review-de-la-soul-and-the-anonymous-nobody/.

173 *Pitchfork* **gave it a 6.4** Nate Patrin, "and the Anonymous Nobody…," *Pitchfork*, September 3, 2016, https://pitchfork.com/reviews/albums/22353 -and-the-anonymous-nobody/.

173 **"an impressive new installment"** Hugh Leask, "De La Soul – And the Anonymous Nobody," *Clash*, August 19, 2016, https://www.clashmusic.com /reviews/de-la-soul-and-the-anonymous-nobody/.

174 *Rolling Stone* **was less complimentary** Alan Light, "Review: De La Soul
Still Pushing Boundaries on 'Anonymous Nobody,'" *Rolling Stone*, August 26,
2016, https://www.rollingstone.com/music/music-album-reviews/review-de-la
-soul-still-pushing-boundaries-on-anonymous-nobody-248448/.

176 **"There was a reaction from the Kickstarter community"** Shawn
Setaro, "How De La Soul Crowdfunded Their New Album With $600K
From Kickstarter," *Forbes*, August 30, 2016, https://www.forbes.com/sites
/shawnsetaro/2016/08/30/de-la-souls-kickstarter-success/?sh=7b3ffd7a72b8.

CHAPTER 10: THE DOVE FLIES

178 **"Catalog is not on Bandcamp"** Kyle Eustice "No, De La Soul's Entire
Catalog Isn't on Bandcamp," *HipHopDX*, September 5, 2018, https://hiphopdx
.com/news/id.48307/title.no-de-la-souls-entire-catalog-isnt-on-bandcamp.

179 **the group wrote on Instagram** De La Soul (@wearedelasoul). 2019.
"Hmmm . . ." Instagram photo, February 25, 2019. https://www.instagram.com
/p/BuUXEsqlCjx/?hl=en.

179 **"Really????"** De La Soul (@wearedelasoul). 2019. "We are being placed
in the line of fire." Instagram photo, February 27, 2019. https://www.instagram
.com/p/BuZHmRVFY1A/?hl=en.

179 **"Feels like they want to silence us to ensure"** De La Soul (@wearedelasoul).
2019. "Your voice is a tool that you sometimes have to use as the weapon to
defend yourself." Instagram photo, February 28, 2019. https://www.instagram
.com/p/Bub1MpMFAYN/?hl=en.

185 **"New day received"** De La Soul (@wearedelasoul). 2021. "Peace . . . New
day received." Instagram photo, March 1, 2021. https://www.instagram.com/p
/CL4jDVmlZUZ/?hl=en.

188 **"a true artist who used music to inspire and uplift others"** De La Soul, "Dear
Dave," *Substack*, March 5, 2023, https://delasoul.substack.com/p/dear-dave.

ABOUT THE AUTHOR

Marcus J. Moore is a music journalist, editor, curator, pundit, professor, and the author of *The Butterfly Effect: How Kendrick Lamar Ignited the Soul of Black America*. He has co-led the jazz-focused "5 Minutes That Will Make You Love . . ." series at the *New York Times*. His work has appeared in *The Atlantic*, NPR, *Pitchfork*, *Time*, *TIDAL*, *GQ*, the *Washington Post*, and *Rolling Stone*.